Empire of Guanduania

By

Bangambiki Habyarimana

Copyright © 2017 Bangambiki Habyarimana

What is Guanduania?

Guanduania is a micronation. The term micronation literally means a small nation. A micronation is an entity that claims to be an independent nation or state but is not officially recognized by world governments or major international organizations. Some micronations are created with serious intent, while others exist as a hobby. The first reference in English to the word micronation in a popular book appears in 1978, the term has since come to be used also retrospectively to refer to earlier unrecognized entities, some of which date to as far back as the 17th century. The concept of a "micronation" is most closely related to cultural nationalism, and can be broken down into three main categories: role playing, social experiments and political simulations. To some, the idea may seem, at face value, childish, ridiculous or even narcissistic, but there exist many micro nationalists who go beyond these negative stereotypes. Not every King or Empress is out for self-glorification.

Micronations should not be confused with internationally recognized but geographically small nations such as Fiji, Monaco, and San Marino, Andorra, etc. for which the term microstate is more commonly used. Micronations generally have several common features:

Micronations may have a form and structure like established sovereign states, including territorial claims, government institutions, official symbols and citizens, albeit on a much smaller scale.

Micronations are often quite small, in both their claimed territory and claimed populations — although there are some exceptions to this rule, with different micronations having different methods of citizenship.

Micronations may issue formal instruments such as postage stamps, coins, banknotes and passports, and confer honors and titles of nobility.

The academic study of micronations and microstates is called 'micropatrology'. The hobby or activity of establishing and operating micronations is known as micronationalism.

So is Guanduania a fantasy nation?

No! Many imaginary countries or nations exist only on the internet or fictional maps. Those countries are active in online communities only and their claims are located on virtual maps or imaginary worlds. The correct definition for those imaginary countries is Geofiction. There are many similarities between Geofiction and micronationalism. Guanduania however, is real-life and it organizes cultural events regularly and all goals and achievements in Guanduania are realistic and executable.

Most micronations are located on the personal property of the founder, but Guanduania is the Universe.

What made you start looking at the Universe in the first place?

Firstly, because we searched for a place that wasn't claimed by any country. We could claim the whole universe for ourselves, since it truly belongs to everyone and to no one. We are a group of people who are concerned about the rights and freedoms of people in the world and beyond. We want to see an end to segregation based on nationality, race, gender, religion, sexual orientation, ethnicity, etc. We want to nullify the negative effects of borders that make people strangers and called aliens in their own universe. We think the universe belongs to us all and that we should have equal rights in it.

Our motto is: "Peace, Love, Justice"!

What actions do you take to raise more attention for equal rights for the citizens of the universe and the preservation of nature?

We're not an organization with enough funds to launch campaigns. Guanduania is a micronation and we remain realistic, but small actions together can make a difference. We send protest letters to governments or companies who violate human rights, endanger peace in the world and destroy the environment or support letters to people and organizations who are in the same struggle as we are. In Guanduania we promote the importance of universe citizenship, of green energy friendly alternatives, recycling, etc. The social media is an important tool for us to share our message.

Are your universal claims legal?

From our view, yes. We were born into this universe and it belongs to us. No law prohibits us to become it's citizen, but many countries have laws that prevent people to travel wherever they want on earth, many people live without official documents, can't find a job, go to school etc because officials refuse to issue necessary documents. We envision a universal country where borders will be abolished, with one democratic constitution, where all people will enjoy the same rights as global citizens. We want to end the economic disparities between the different parts of the world. We want the citizens of the universe benefit equally from what nature has to offer, it shouldn't be the privilege of a tiny minority.

Which countries have established diplomatic ties with Guanduania?

Guanduania has not sought to establish formal bilateral relations with any other state, and does not intend to do so. Our message is more important than our self-declared sovereignty. But Guanduania is worldwide active in the micronational community and it intends to sign treaties of friendship and mutual recognition with other micronations.

What are the Politics of Guanduania?

We are a democratic constitutional monarchy, where all the power comes from the people as stated in the guanduanian constitution.

What is the population of Guanduania?

As of 02 August 2017, Guanduania had a population of 4 citizens.

How can I become a Guanduanian?

Send us a message through our site at www.guanduania.org

Guanduania

The Empire of Guanduania is a micronation founded on 27 Jul 2017 by Emperor Justus I of Guanduania . Guanduania claims the whole universe as it's legitimate territory. The capital of the empire is Guanduanis and its national anthem is Beloved Motherland.

National Heroes of Guanduania

Heather Heyer (1985-2017) was a civil rights activist killed while opposing a white supremacist rally, the "Unite the Right Rally" in Charlottesville, Virginia on August 12, 2017. On August 16, 2017 Guanduania's Emperor Justus I of Guanduania declared her a national hero for her efforts to stop hate and racism in America and in the world. Guanduania declared the day Heather Heyer died as a national holiday to remember her and those who risk their lives every day to promote a world free of all kinds of discrimination.

Guanduanis

Guanduanis is the capital city of the Empire of Guanduania and seat of power of its Emperor Justus I of Guanduania. The city is the historical and cultural center of Guanduania, being the site of its foundation in 2017.

Foreign Relations of Guanduania

Foreign relations of Guanduania are open with any nation that they share common values. Agreements with other states or with international organizations are concluded by the Government.

Conduct of foreign relations is stated in Chapter 10 of the Guanduanian Constitution

Who is a Guanduanian?

Guanduanians are citizens of Guanduania. It's a new race of men who understand all men are heirs of this universe and should live and let others live with equal rights.

Religions in Guanduania

Guanduanians holds various beliefs. Each Guanduanian is free to hold whatever belief he/she wants. Guanduanians respect different beliefs and do not segregate people based on them or other differences. Nonetheless Guanduanians don't tolerate beliefs that encourage to cause physical or psychological harm to other Guanduanians.

Eternal Love Church

The Eternal Love Church was founded on 28 May 2016 by The Most Reverend Bangambiki Habyarimana who later took the name of Emperor Justus I of Guanduania after founding the Empire of Guanduania on 20 July 2017. The Eternal Love Church faith is the most practiced religious belief in Guanduania. Guanduania is a tolerant society; the Guanduanians accept in their midst people from different faiths and Guanduania has no official religion or State Church. Though the Emperor Justus I of Guanduania is the Primate of the Eternal Love Church, all religions are accepted and protected under the Constitution of Guanduania. The church is headquartered in Guanduanis, the empire's capital.

Constitution of Guanduania

The Constitution of the Empire of Guanduania is the fundamental law of the land. It was adopted by Parliament on the 02 of August 2017, which was declared one of Guanduania's national holidays.

National Anthem Beloved Motherland

Beloved Motherland is the national anthem of the Empire of Guanduania.

Lyrics

In love of all your children
Beautiful motherland of those who dare to fight
Guanduania, your name is freedom
The Sun of peace forever will shine

Chorus: (2x) Guanduania, our Glorious Land
Stone by stone building a new hope
Millions of hands joined for one goal
O Loved motherland we will succeed

United people from one end of the land to the other
We harvest the fruits of the combat for Peace
For Love and for Justice
Hoping for a better tomorrow

We will fight with the sword of truth
Against all type of injustice
We will defend our freedoms at all costs
Even give our lives to defend it.

Etymology

Guanduania means golden star in Guanduanian, a nation destined to shine among the nations.

History of Guanduania

Though Guanduania was founded in 2017, it had existed since the foundation of the world. It incarnated the forces of good that fought against the forces of evil. Guanduanians have existed all along since the beginning. Guanduanians are those people who are born good, resist evil at all times and help humanity come off the cliff when everything seems lost. They were the heroes of the past who pulled their tribes and nations off the brink, who protected their family from calamity, they are those who sacrificed their own lives for the greater good of humanity. Those have existed in every country on earth, they were inhabited by the spirit of Guanduania, the Golden Star.

King Justus I of Guanduania, in consolidating Guanduania as an Empire wanted to streamline the efforts of those men and women of good against the forces of evil that besiege humanity. It goes without saying, everybody knows it when they turn on their TVs and Radio or browse their news feeds. Guanduania comes as the solution human kind has been waiting for, a new Messiah Empire that will bring back the Peace, Love and Justice all human beings thirst for.

Guanduania declared its existence on 27 July 2017.

Guanduania is an independent State, a state of mind that claims no one's territory as it has it's own natural territory viz the Universe. The aim of Guanduania is to promote peace, love and justice in the world fighting against all injustices and discriminations.

The Empire of Guanduania is a Constitutional Monarchy ruled by the House of Justus. The Constitution of Guanduania was officially promulgated on 02 August 2017 by Emperor Justus I of Guanduania.

Besides members of the royal house, on 05/August 2017the Emperor of Guanduania granted citizenship to the third guanduanian citizen.

On August 7, 2017 For the Emperor addresses the nation for the first time

On 16 August 2017 the Emperor Justus I of Guanduania, appointed by decree Lady Heather Heyer to the Most Honorable Order of the Golden Key.

Factsheet

Full Name: The Empire of Guanduania

Common Name: Guanduania

Demonym: Guanduanian

Population: 4

Total Area: Whole Universe

Government Type: Constitutional Monarchy

Head of State: His Imperial Majesty Emperor Justus I of Guanduania

Head of Government: Her Royal Highness Princess Justina

Capital: Guanduanis

Motto: "Pax Caritas Iustitia" (Peace Charity Justice)

Currencies: The Guanduanian Crown

Anthem: Beloved Motherland

Capital city: Guanduanis

Largest city: Kandlamana

Official language(s): Guanduanian

Official religion(s): Guanduania has no official religion, citizens have the freedom to choose the religion they want or no religion at all. The most practiced religion is Christianity represented by The Eternal Love Church of Guanduania

Demonym: Guanduanian

Government: Constitutional Monarchy

Emperor : Emperor Justus I of Guanduania

Legislature: Parliament of Guanduania

Established: 27 July 2017

Area claimed: Infinite

National sport: Football

National dish: Zinklunt

National drink: Tea

National animal : Royal Lion

National Tree   Ficus thonningii

National Bird   Dove

Patron saint: St Gwanzilka

Official Website: www.guanduania.org

Government and Politics

The Empire of Guanduania is a Constitutional Monarchy ruled by the House of Justus. The Constitution of Guanduania was officially promulgated on 02 August 2017 by Emperor Justus I of Guanduania

The government is led by the prime minister from the party that has the majority in parliament.

Legislative powers are vested in Parliament whose members are voted by direct popular vote

The administration of justice is vested in the independent judiciary.

The duties of the monarchy under the Constitution

Under the Constitution of Guanduania

The Emperor/Empress remains the head of state.

The Emperor/Empress opens Parliament.

Members of the government shall regularly report to the Emperor/Empress about the current events in the country.

Emperor/Empress is Chairman of the Advisory Committee on international questions. This Committee is elected by Parliament for consultation between the government and Parliament on foreign policy.

The Emperor/Empress has the highest military rank: he is a full General and full Admiral. But the army is subject only to the government.

As head of state the Emperor/Empress accepts credentials from foreign diplomats and signs the credentials from foreign ambassadors.

The Emperor/Empress has immunity, i.e., cannot be held accountable for their actions in accordance with the criminal law. However, he/she can be sued in court in accordance with the civil law.

Each year Parliament decides what amount will be allocated to the king to perform his/her duties.

He/she is a non-political head of state, a national symbol.

Holidays in Guanduania

These are official holidays in the Empire of Guanduania. These days are very important to the guanduanian people, in them we remember what we hold dear in our hearts and by them we show what are our values as a nation.

Freedom Day
1 January

Heroes Day
5 January

No Plastic Bag Day
10 January

Day against xenophobia
15 January

Day of the global citizen
20 January

Day against tribalism
25 January

LGBT day
30 January

Day against religious extremism
25 January

World Cancer Day
2 February

Justice
15 February

International Human Solidarity Day
20 February

Education Day
25 February

Youth Day
27 February

Nature's Day
5 March

World Malaria Day
26 April

Freedom of Expression Day
15 May

Family Day
30 May

No-Tobacco Day
1 June

Child Labor
15 June

Refugee Day
26 June

Victims of Torture
30 June

Constitution Day
15 July

Independence Day
27 July

Flag Day
30 July

Constitution Day
02 August

Heather Heyer Day
12 August

Day of Charity
1 September

Democracy
15 September

Total Elimination of Nuclear Weapons
25 September

Older Persons
1 October

Orphans Day
7 October

Eradication of Poverty
22 October

Persons with Disabilities
20 December

Anti-Corruption Day
28 December

Human Rights Day
30 December

Ten Commandments for Guanduanians

Though shalt live and let live

Though shalt consider all human being as thy brother or sister

Though shalt pursue peace to the end

Though shalt resist injustice by non-violent means

Though shalt defend your rights as a world citizen by all your forces

Though shalt avoid all kinds of discrimination in your life-religious, racial, sexual orientation, disabilities, gender, age, political, etc.

Though shalt resist all extremist behavior

Though shalt not take advantage of the weak, though shalt instead give him/ her a hand

Though shalt respect the law

Though shalt respect nature

National Symbols

The Flag

The current flag of Guanduania was adopted on July 2, 2017 which will henceforth be celebrated as Flag Day. The red symbolizes the determination the guanduanians have to defend their freedom, even dying for it if necessary. The red also symbolizes the blood of all those unsung heroes who lost their lives defending the freedoms we as guanduanians enjoy now.

The blue represents the hope guanduanians they have in a better future.

Yellow represents prosperity

White represents peace and the crossed golden keys represent freedom by which peace, love, justice, prosperity are unlocked.

Coat of Arms of Guanduania

The book represents education, the foundation of all enlightened society. The two swords represent the sword of truth by which we fight all evil. The lion and crown represent His Imperial Majesty, the golden star represent one prosperous guanduanian people. The Keys represent liberty, by which all development is possible.

National mammal is the lion, symbol of strength and confidence.

National bird is the dove, symbol of peace

The national tree is the Ficus thonningii, a tall big shady tree, long lasting, symbolizing the empire of Guanduania; a nation big enough and strong enough to shelter all its children.

Guanduania and the Law

The Empire of Guanduania is absolutely legal. Under international law, the Montevideo Convention on Rights and Duties of States sets out the criteria for statehood in article 1. It says: "The state as a person of international law should possess the following qualifications: (a) a permanent population; (b) a defined territory; (c) government; and (d) capacity to enter into relations with the other states."

The Montevideo Convention carries on to say in article 3, "The political existence of the state is independent of recognition by the other states" Under these guidelines, bodies that meet the criteria outlined in article 1 of the Montevideo Convention on Rights and Duties of States can be regarded as sovereign under international law. This would not matter whether other nations or organizations have recognized the micro nation or not.

The King's First Speech

To all citizens and friends of Guanduania,

We wish you peace and prosperity and call you to participate in this great endeavor to make the world a better place than it is today. We cannot sleep while there is still injustice around us, while war still kills innocent civilians, while citizens continue to flee their homes, while borders continue to be closed to desperate asylum seekers, while people are being targeted for their race, tribe, creed, sexual orientation, political views, etc.

We are the future of this world, let us rise up and make a difference.

Long live freedom, peace, justice and love for our neighbor in the world
Long live sustainable development
Long live Guanduania, the Empire of Peace.

HIM Emperor Justus I of Guanduania.

Order of the Golden Key

The Order of the Golden Key is the highest honor the state of Guanduania can bestow on an individual who has shown exceptional love and service to Guanduania or the world.

The first ever person to receive this honor was Heather Heyer, an American civil rights activist who was murdered while she opposed a white supremacist rally in Charlottesville on 12 August 2016. She was inducted in the order by decree on 16 August 2017 by HIM Justus I of Guanduania.

Constitution of Guanduania 2017

The Instrument of Government

Chapter Basic principles of the form of government

Art 1

All public power in Guanduania proceeds from the people.

Guanduanian democracy is founded on the free formation of opinion and on universal and equal suffrage. It is realized through a representative and parliamentary form of government and through local self-government.

Public power is exercised under the law.

Art 2

Public power shall be exercised with respect for the equal worth of all and the liberty and dignity of the individual. The personal, economic and cultural welfare of the individual shall be fundamental aims of public activity. In particular, the public institutions shall secure the right to employment, housing and education, and shall promote social care and social security, as well as favorable conditions for good health.

The public institutions shall promote sustainable development leading to a good environment for present and future generations.

The public institutions shall promote the ideals of democracy as guidelines in all sectors of society and protect the private and family lives of the individual.

The public institutions shall promote the opportunity for all to attain participation and equality in society and for the rights of the child to be safeguarded. The public institutions shall combat discrimination of persons on grounds of gender, color, national or ethnic origin, linguistic or religious affiliation, functional disability, sexual orientation, age or other circumstance affecting the individual.

The opportunities of ethnic, linguistic and religious minorities to preserve and develop a cultural and social life of their own shall be promoted.

Art 3

The Instrument of Government, the Act of Succession, the Freedom of the Press Act and the Fundamental Law on Freedom of Expression are the fundamental laws of the Realm.

Art 4

The Guanduanian Parliament is the foremost representative of the people.

The Guanduanian Parliament enacts the laws, determines State taxes and decides how State funds shall be employed. The Guanduanian Parliament shall examine the government and administration of the Realm.

Art 5

The Emperor or Queen who occupies the throne of Guanduania in accordance with the Act of Succession shall be the Head of State.

Art 6

The Government governs the Realm. It is accountable to the Guanduanian Parliament

Art 7

Guanduania has local authorities at local and regional level.

Art 8

Courts of law exist for the administration of justice, and central and local government administrative authorities exist for public administration.

Art 9

Courts of law, administrative authorities and others performing public administration functions shall pay regard in their work to the equality of all before the law and shall observe objectivity and impartiality.

Chapter 2 Fundamental rights and freedoms

Part 1 Freedom of opinion

Art 1

Everyone shall be guaranteed the following rights and freedoms in his or her relations with the public institutions:

Freedom of expression: that is, the freedom to communicate information and express thoughts, opinions and sentiments, whether orally, pictorially, in writing, or in any other way;
Freedom of information: that is, the freedom to procure and receive information and otherwise acquaint oneself with the utterances of others;
Freedom of assembly: that is, the freedom to organize or attend meetings for the purposes of information or the expression of opinion or for any other similar purpose, or for the purpose of presenting artistic work;
Freedom to demonstrate: that is, the freedom to organize or take part in demonstrations in a public place;
Freedom of association: that is, the freedom to associate with others for public or private purposes; and
Freedom of worship: that is, the freedom to practice one's religion alone or in the company of others.

The provisions of the Freedom of the Press Act and the Fundamental Law on Freedom of Expression shall apply concerning the freedom of the press and the corresponding freedom of expression on sound radio, television and certain similar transmissions, as well as in films, video recordings, sound recordings and other technical recordings.

The Freedom of the Press Act also contains provisions concerning the right of access to official documents.

Art 2

No one shall in his or her relations with the public institutions be coerced to divulge an opinion in a political, religious, cultural or other such connection. Nor may anyone in his or her relations with the public institutions be coerced to participate in a meeting for the shaping of opinion or a demonstration or other manifestation of opinion, or to belong to a political association, religious community or other association for opinion referred to in sentence one.

Art 3

No record in a public register concerning a Guanduanian citizen may be based without his or her consent solely on his or her political opinions.

Part 2 Physical integrity and freedom of movement

Art 4

There shall be no capital punishment.

Art 5

Everyone shall be protected against corporal punishment. No one may be subjected to torture or medical intervention with the purpose of extorting or suppressing statements.

Art 6

Everyone shall be protected in their relations with the public institutions against any physical violation also in cases other than cases under Articles 4 and 5. Everyone shall likewise be protected against body searches, house searches and other such invasions of privacy, against examination of mail or other confidential correspondence, and against eavesdropping and the recording of telephone conversations or other confidential communications.

In addition to what is laid down in paragraph one, everyone shall be protected in their relations with the public institutions against significant invasions of their personal privacy, if these occur without their consent and involve the surveillance or systematic monitoring of the individual's personal circumstances.

Art 7

No Guanduanian citizen may be deported from or refused entry into the Realm.

No Guanduanian citizen who is domiciled in the Realm or who has previously been domiciled in the Realm may be deprived of his or her citizenship. It may however be prescribed that children under the age of eighteen shall have the same nationality as their parents or as one parent.

Art 8

Everyone shall be protected in their relations with the public institutions against deprivations of personal liberty. All Guanduanian citizens shall also in other respects be guaranteed freedom of movement within the Realm and freedom to depart the Realm.

Part 3 Rule of law

Art 9

If a public authority other than a court of law has deprived an individual of his or her liberty on account of a criminal act or because he or she is suspected of having committed such an act, the individual shall be entitled to have the deprivation of liberty examined before a court of law without undue delay. This shall not, however, apply where the matter concerns the transfer to Guanduania of responsibility for executing a penal sanction involving deprivation of liberty according to a sentence in another state.

Also those who for reasons other than those specified in paragraph one, have been taken forcibly into custody, shall likewise be entitled to have the matter of custody examined before a court of law without undue delay. In such a case, examination before a tribunal shall be equated with examination before a court of law provided the composition of the tribunal has been laid down in law and it is stipulated that the chair of the tribunal shall be currently, or shall have been previously, a permanent salaried judge.

If examination has not been referred to an authority which is competent under paragraph one or two, such examination shall be undertaken by a court of general jurisdiction.

Art 10

No one may be sentenced to a penalty or penal sanction for an act which was not subject to a penal sanction at the time it was committed. Nor may anyone be sentenced to a penal sanction which is more severe than that which was in force when the act was committed. The provisions laid down here with respect to penal sanctions also apply to forfeiture and other special legal effects of crime.

No taxes or charges due the State may be imposed except inasmuch as this follows from provisions which were in force when the circumstance arose which occasioned the liability for the tax or charge. Should the Guanduanian Parliament find that special reasons so warrant, it may however lay down in law that taxes or charges due the State shall be imposed even though no such act had entered into force when the aforementioned circumstance arose, provided the Government, or a committee of the Guanduanian Parliament, had submitted a proposal to this effect to the Guanduanian Parliament at the time concerned. A written communication from the Government to the Guanduanian Parliament announcing the forthcoming introduction of such a proposal is equated with a formal proposal. The Guanduanian Parliament may furthermore prescribe that exceptions shall be made to the provisions of sentence one if it considers that this is warranted on special grounds connected with war, the danger of war, or grave economic crisis.

Art 11

No court of law may be established on account of an act already committed, or for a particular dispute or otherwise for a particular case.

Legal proceedings are to be carried out fairly and within a reasonable period of time. Proceedings in courts of law shall be open to the public.

Part 4 Protection against discrimination

Art 12

No act of law or other provision may imply the unfavorable treatment of anyone because they belong to a minority group by reason of ethnic origin, color, or other similar circumstances or on account of their sexual orientation.

Art 13

No act of law or other provision may imply the unfavorable treatment of anyone on grounds of gender, unless the provision forms part of efforts to promote equality between men and women or relates to compulsory military service or other equivalent official duties.

Art 14

A trade union or an employer or employers' association shall be entitled to take industrial action unless otherwise provided in an act of law or under an agreement.

Part 5 Protection of property and the right of public access

Art 15

The property of every individual shall be so guaranteed that no one may be compelled by expropriation or other such disposition to surrender property to the public institutions or to a private subject, or tolerate restriction by the public institutions of the use of land or buildings, other than where necessary to satisfy pressing public interests.

A person who is compelled to surrender property by expropriation or other such disposition shall be guaranteed full compensation for his or her loss. Compensation shall also be guaranteed to a person whose use of land or buildings is restricted by the public institutions in such a manner that on-going land use in the affected part of the property is substantially impaired, or injury results which is significant in relation to the value of that part of the property. Compensation shall be determined according to principles laid down in law.

In the case of limitations on the use of land or buildings on grounds of protection of human health or the environment, or on grounds of safety, however, the rules laid down in law apply in the matter of entitlement to compensation.

Everyone shall have access to the natural environment in accordance with the right of public access, notwithstanding the above provisions.

Part 6 Copyright

Art 16

Authors, artists and photographers shall own the rights to their works in accordance with rules laid down in law.

Part 7 Freedom of trade

Art 17

Limitations affecting the right to trade or practice a profession may be introduced only in order to protect pressing public interests and never solely in order to further the economic interests of a particular person or enterprise.

Part 8 Education and research

Art 18

All children covered by compulsory schooling shall be entitled to a free basic education in the public education system. The public institutions shall be responsible also for the provision of higher education.

The freedom of research is protected according to rules laid down in law.

Art 19

To the extent provided for in Articles 21 to 24, the following rights and freedoms may be limited in law:

   1. Freedom of expression, freedom of information, freedom of assembly, freedom to demonstrate and freedom of association (Article 1, points 1 to 5);
   2. Protection against any physical violation in cases other than cases under Articles 4 and 5, against body searches, house searches and other such invasions of privacy, against violations of confidential items of mail or communications and otherwise against violations involving surveillance and monitoring of the individual's personal circumstances (Article 6);
   3. Freedom of movement (Article 8); and
   4. Public court proceedings (Article 11, paragraph two, sentence two).

With authority in law, the rights and freedoms referred to in paragraph one may be limited by other statute in cases under Chapter 8, Article 5, and in respect of prohibition of the disclosure of matters which have come to a person's knowledge in the performance of public or official duties. Freedom of assembly and freedom to demonstrate may similarly be limited also in cases under Article 24, paragraph one, sentence two.

Art 21

The limitations referred to in Article 20 may be imposed only to satisfy a purpose acceptable in a democratic society. The limitation must never go beyond what is necessary with regard to the purpose which occasioned it, nor may it be carried so far as to constitute a threat to the free shaping of opinion as one of the fundaments of democracy. No limitation may be imposed solely on grounds of a political, religious, cultural or other such opinion.

Art 22

A draft law under Article 20 shall be held in abeyance, unless rejected by the Guanduanian Parliament, for a minimum of twelve months from the date on which the first Guanduanian Parliament committee report on the proposal was submitted to the Chamber, if so moved by at least ten members. The Guanduanian Parliament may, however, adopt the proposal directly if it has the support of at least five sixths of those voting.

Paragraph one shall not apply to any draft law prolonging the life of a law for a period not exceeding two years. Nor shall it apply to any draft law concerned only with:

1. Prohibition of the disclosure of matters which have come to a person's knowledge in the performance of public or official duties, where secrecy is called for with regard to interests under Chapter 2, Article 2 of the Freedom of the Press Act;
2. House searches and similar invasions of privacy; or
3. Deprivation of liberty as a penal sanction for a specific act. The Committee on the Constitution determines on behalf of the Guanduanian Parliament whether paragraph one applies in respect of a particular draft law.

Art 23

Freedom of expression and freedom of information may be limited with regard to the security of the Realm, the national supply of goods, public order and public safety, the good repute of the individual, the sanctity of private life, and the prevention and prosecution of crime. Freedom of expression may also be limited in business activities. Freedom of expression and freedom of information may otherwise be limited only where particularly important grounds so warrant.

In judging what limitations may be introduced in accordance with paragraph one, particular attention must be paid to the importance of the widest possible freedom of expression and freedom of information in political, religious, professional, scientific and cultural matters.

The adoption of provisions which regulate in more detail a particular manner of disseminating or receiving information, without regard to its content, shall not be deemed a limitation of the freedom of expression or the freedom of information.

Art 24

Freedom of assembly and freedom to demonstrate may be limited in the interests of preserving public order and public safety at a meeting or demonstration, or with regard to the circulation of traffic. These freedoms may otherwise be limited only with regard to the security of the Realm or in order to combat an epidemic.

Freedom of association may be limited only in respect of organizations whose activities are of a military or quasi-military nature, or constitute persecution of a population group on grounds of ethnic origin, color, or other such conditions.

Art 25

For foreign nationals within the Realm, special limitations may be introduced to the following rights and freedoms:

1. Freedom of expression, freedom of information, freedom of assembly, freedom to demonstrate, freedom of association and freedom of worship (Article 1, paragraph one);
2. Protection against coercion to divulge an opinion (Article 2, sentence one);
3. protection against physical violations also in cases other than cases under Articles 4 and 5, against body searches, house searches and other such invasions of privacy, against violations of

confidential items of mail or communications and otherwise against violations involving surveillance and monitoring of the individual's personal circumstances (Article 6);

    4. protection against deprivation of liberty (Article 8, sentence one);

    5. the right to have a deprivation of liberty other than a deprivation of liberty on account of a criminal act or on suspicion of having committed such an act examined before a court of law (Article 9, paragraphs two and three);

    6. public court proceedings (Article 11, paragraph two, sentence two);

    7. Authors', artists' and photographers' rights to their works (Article 16);

    8. the right to trade or practice a profession (Article 17);

    9. the right to freedom of research (Article 18, paragraph two); and

    10. protection against violations on grounds of an opinion (Article 21, sentence three).

The provisions of Article 22, paragraph one, paragraph two, sentence one and paragraph three shall apply with respect to the special limitations referred to in paragraph one.

Chapter 3 The Guanduanian Parliament

Part 1 Formation and composition of the Guanduanian Parliament

Art 1

The Guanduanian Parliament is appointed by means of free, secret and direct elections.

Voting in such elections is by party, with an option for the voter to express a personal preference vote.

Party denotes any association or group of voters which runs for election under a particular designation.

Art 2

The Guanduanian Parliament consists of a single chamber comprising 2 members. Alternates shall be appointed for members.

Part 2 Ordinary elections

Art 3

Ordinary elections to the Guanduanian Parliament are held every four years.

Part 3 Right to vote and eligibility to stand for election

Art 4

Every Guanduanian citizen who is currently domiciled within the Realm or who has ever been domiciled within the Realm, and who has reached the age of eighteen, is entitled to vote in an election to the Guanduanian Parliament.

Only a person who is entitled to vote may be a member or alternate member of the Guanduanian Parliament.

The question of whether a person has the right to vote is determined on the basis of an electoral roll drawn up prior to the election.

Part 4 Constituencies

Art 5

The Realm is divided up into constituencies for the purpose of elections to the Guanduanian Parliament.

Part 5 Distribution of seats among constituencies

Art 6

Of the seats in the Guanduanian Parliament, 2 are fixed constituency seats and 0 are adjustment seats.

The fixed constituency seats are distributed among the constituencies on the basis of a calculation of the relationship between the number of persons entitled to vote in each constituency, and the total number of persons entitled to vote throughout the whole of the Realm. The distribution of seats among the constituencies is determined for four years at a time.

Part 6 Distribution of seats among parties

Art 7

The seats are distributed among parties.

Only parties which receive at least four per cent of the votes cast throughout the Realm may be included in the distribution of seats. A party receiving fewer votes, however, participates in the distribution of the fixed constituency seats in a constituency in which it receives at least twelve per cent of the votes cast.

Art 8

The fixed constituency seats in each constituency are distributed proportionately among the parties on the basis of the election result in that constituency.

The adjustment seats are distributed among the parties in such a way that the distribution of all the seats in the Guanduanian Parliament, other than those fixed constituency seats which have been allocated to a party polling less than four per cent of the national vote, is in proportion to the total number of votes cast throughout the Realm for the respective parties participating in the distribution of seats. If, in the distribution of the fixed constituency seats, a party obtains seats which exceed the number corresponding to the proportional representation of that party in the Guanduanian Parliament, then that party and the fixed constituency seats which it has obtained are disregarded in distributing the adjustment seats. The adjustment seats are allocated to constituencies after they have been distributed among the parties.

The odd-number method is used to distribute the seats among the parties, with the first divisor adjusted to 1.4.

Art 9

One member is appointed for each seat a party obtains, together with an alternate for that member.

Part 7 Electoral period

Art 10

Each election is valid for the period from the date on which the newly-elected Guanduanian Parliament convenes to the date on which the Guanduanian Parliament elected next thereafter convenes.

The newly-elected Guanduanian Parliament convenes on the fifteenth day following Election Day but no sooner than the fourth day after the result of the election has been declared.

Part 8 Extraordinary elections

Art 11

The Government may decide that an extraordinary election to the Guanduanian Parliament is to be held between ordinary elections. An extraordinary election is held within three months from the decision.

After an election to the Guanduanian Parliament has been held, the Government may not hold an extraordinary election until three months from the date on which the newly-elected Guanduanian Parliament first convened. Neither may the Government decide to hold an extraordinary election while ministers remain at their posts, after all have been formally discharged, pending assumption of office by a new Government.

Rules concerning an extraordinary election in a particular case are laid down in Chapter 6, Article 5.

Part 9 Appeals against election results

Art 12

Appeals against elections to the Guanduanian Parliament shall be lodged with an Election Review Board appointed by the Guanduanian Parliament. There is no right of appeal against a decision of the Board.

A person who has been elected a member of the Guanduanian Parliament exercises his or her mandate even if the election result has been appealed. If the result of the election is revised, a new member takes his or her seat immediately after the revised result has been declared. This applies in a similar manner to alternate members.

The Election Review Board consists of a chair, who is currently, or has been previously, a permanent salaried judge and who may not be a member of the Guanduanian Parliament, and six other members. The members are elected after each ordinary election, as soon as the result of the election becomes final, and serve until a new election for the Board is held. The chair is elected separately.

Part 10 Further rules

Art 13

Further rules concerning matters under Article 1, paragraph three and Articles 3 to 12 and concerning the appointment of alternates for members of the Guanduanian Parliament are laid down in the Guanduanian Parliament Act or elsewhere in law.

Chapter 4 The work of the Guanduanian Parliament

Part 1 Guanduanian Parliament session

Art 1

The Guanduanian Parliament convenes in session every year. Sessions are held in Guanduanis, unless otherwise determined by the Guanduanian Parliament or the Speaker, with regard to the liberty or safety of parliament.

Part 2.The Speaker

Art 2

The Guanduanian Parliament elects a Speaker and First, Second, and Third Deputy Speakers from among its members for each electoral period.

Part 3 Guanduanian Parliament committees

Art 3

The Guanduanian Parliament elects committees from among its members in accordance with rules laid down in the Guanduanian Parliament Act. These shall include a Committee on the Constitution and a Committee on Finance.

Part 4 Right to introduce proposals

Art 4

The Government and every member of the Guanduanian Parliament has the right to introduce proposals on any matter coming within the jurisdiction of the Guanduanian Parliament, in accordance with provisions laid down in the Guanduanian Parliament Act, unless otherwise provided in the present Instrument of Government.

Part 5 Preparation of matters

Art 5

Any matter raised by the Government or by a member of the Guanduanian Parliament shall be prepared by a committee before it is settled, unless otherwise provided in the present Instrument of Government.

Part 6 Settlement of matters

Art 6

When a matter comes up for decision in the Chamber, every member of the Guanduanian Parliament and every minister has the right to speak in accordance with more detailed rules laid down in the Guanduanian Parliament Act.

Rules concerning grounds for disqualification are also laid down in the Guanduanian Parliament Act.

Art 7

When a vote is taken in the Chamber, the opinion supported by more than half of those voting constitutes the decision of the Guanduanian Parliament, unless otherwise provided in the present Instrument of Government or, in the case of matters relating to Guanduanian Parliament procedure, in a principal provision of the Guanduanian Parliament Act. Rules concerning the procedure to be followed in the event of a tied vote are laid down in the Guanduanian Parliament Act.

Part 7 Follow-up and evaluation

Art 8

Each committee follows up and evaluates decisions of the Guanduanian Parliament within the committee's subject area.

Part 8 Openness in the Chamber

Art 9

Meetings of the Chamber are open to the public. A meeting may, nevertheless, be held behind closed doors in accordance with rules laid down in the Guanduanian Parliament Act.

Part 9 Members' legal status

Art 10

Members of the Guanduanian Parliament or alternates for such members may exercise their mandate as members notwithstanding any official duty or other similar obligation.

Art 11

Members of the Guanduanian Parliament or alternates for such members may not resign their mandate without the Guanduanian Parliament's consent.

Where there are grounds, the Election Review Board shall examine on its own initiative whether a particular member or an alternate is eligible under Chapter 3, Article 4, and paragraph two. A person pronounced to be ineligible is thereby deprived of his or her mandate.

Members or alternates may be deprived of their mandate in cases other than cases under paragraph two only if they have proved themselves manifestly unfit to hold a mandate by reason of a criminal act. A decision in such a case shall be taken by a court of law.

Art 12

Legal proceedings may not be initiated against a person who holds a mandate as a member of the Guanduanian Parliament, or who has held such a mandate, on account of a statement or an act made in the exercise of his or her mandate, unless the Guanduanian Parliament has given its consent thereto in a decision supported by at least five sixths of those voting.

Nor may such a person be deprived of his or her liberty, or restricted from travelling within the Realm, on account of an act or statement made in the exercise of his or her mandate, unless the Guanduanian Parliament has given such consent thereto.

If, in any other case, a member of the Guanduanian Parliament is suspected of having committed a criminal act, the relevant legal provisions concerning apprehension, arrest or detention are applied only if he or she admits guilt or was caught in the act, or the minimum penalty for the offence is imprisonment for two years.

Art 13

During such time as a member is acting as Speaker of the Guanduanian Parliament or is a member of the Government, his or her mandate as a member shall be exercised by an alternate. The Guanduanian Parliament may stipulate in the Guanduanian Parliament Act that an alternate shall replace a member when he or she is on leave of absence.

The rules laid down in Articles 10 and 12, paragraph one also apply to the Speaker and the Speaker's mandate.

The rules relating to a member of the Guanduanian Parliament apply also to an alternate exercising a mandate as a member.

Part 10 Further rules

Art 14

Further rules concerning the work of the Guanduanian Parliament are laid down in the Guanduanian Parliament Act.

Chapter 5 The Head of State

Art 1

Chapter 1, Article 5 states that the Emperor or Queen who occupies the throne of Guanduania in accordance with the Act of Succession is the Head of State.

Art 2

Only a person who is a Guanduanian citizen and who has reached the age of eighteen may serve as Head of State. The Head of State may not at the same time be a minister, hold the office of Speaker or serve as a member of the Guanduanian Parliament.

Art 3

The Head of State shall be kept informed by the Prime Minister concerning the affairs of the Realm. The Government convenes as Council of State under the chairmanship of the Head of State when required.

The Head of State shall consult the Prime Minister before undertaking travel abroad.

Art 4

If the Emperor or Queen who is Head of State is not in a position to perform his or her duties, the member of the Royal House in line under the order of succession and able to do so shall assume and perform the duties of Head of State in the capacity of Regent ad interim.

Art 5

Should the Royal House become extinct, the Guanduanian Parliament elects a Regent to perform the duties of Head of State until further notice. The Guanduanian Parliament elects a Deputy Regent at the same time.

The same applies if the Emperor or Queen who is Head of State dies or abdicates and the heir to the throne has not yet reached the age of eighteen.

Art 6

If the Emperor or Queen who is Head of State has been prevented for six consecutive months from performing his or her duties, or has failed to perform his or her duties, the Government shall notify the matter to the Guanduanian Parliament. The Guanduanian Parliament decides whether the Emperor or Queen shall be deemed to have abdicated.

Art 7

The Guanduanian Parliament may elect a person to serve as Regent ad interim under a Government order when no one competent under Article 4 or 5 is in a position to serve.

The Speaker, or, in his or her absence, one of the Deputy Speakers, serves as Regent ad interim under a Government order when no other competent person is in a position to serve.

Art 8

The Emperor or Queen who is Head of State cannot be prosecuted for his or her actions. Nor can a Regent be prosecuted for his or her actions as Head of State.

Chapter 6 The Government

Part 1 Composition of the Government

Art 1

The Government consists of the Prime Minister and other ministers.

The Prime Minister is appointed in accordance with the rules laid down in Articles 4 to 6. The Prime Minister appoints the other ministers.

Art 2

The ministers must be Guanduanian citizens. A minister may not have any other employment.
Neither may he or she hold any appointment or engage in any activity which might impair public
confidence in him or her.

Part 2 Vote on the Prime Minister after an election

Art 3

No later than two weeks after it has convened, a newly- elected Guanduanian Parliament shall
determine by means of a vote whether the Prime Minister has sufficient support in the Guanduanian
Parliament. If more than half of the members of the Guanduanian Parliament vote no, the Prime
Minister shall be discharged. No vote shall be held if the Prime Minister has already been
discharged.

Part 3 Formation of the Government

Art 4

When a Prime Minister is to be appointed, the Speaker summons for consultation representatives
from each party group in the Guanduanian Parliament. The Speaker confers with the Deputy
Speakers before presenting a proposal to the Guanduanian Parliament. The Guanduanian Parliament
shall vote on the proposal within four days, without prior preparation in committee. If more than
half the members of the Guanduanian Parliament vote against the proposal, it is rejected. In any
other case, it is adopted.

Art 5

If the Guanduanian Parliament rejects the Speaker's proposal, the procedure laid down in Article 4 is
repeated. If the Guanduanian Parliament rejects the Speaker's proposal four times, the procedure
for appointing a Prime Minister is abandoned and resumed only after an election to the
Guanduanian Parliament has been held. If no ordinary election is due in any case to be held within
three months, an extraordinary election shall be held within the same space of time.

Art 6

When the Guanduanian Parliament has approved a proposal for a new Prime Minister, the Prime
Minister shall inform the Guanduanian Parliament as soon as possible of the names of the ministers.
Government changes hands thereafter at a Council of State before the Head of State or, in his or her
absence, before the Speaker. The Speaker is always summoned to attend such a Council.

The Speaker issues a letter of appointment for the Prime Minister on the Guanduanian Parliament's
behalf.

Part 4 Discharge of the Prime Minister or a minister

Art 7

If the Guanduanian Parliament declares that the Prime Minister, or a member of his or her Government, no longer has its confidence, the Speaker shall discharge the minister concerned. However, if the Government is in a position to order an extraordinary election to the Guanduanian Parliament and does so within one week from a declaration of no confidence, the minister shall not be discharged.

Rules concerning discharge of the Prime Minister following a vote on the Prime Minister after an election are laid down in Article 3.

Art 8

A minister shall be discharged if he or she so requests; in such a case the Prime Minister is discharged by the Speaker, and any other minister by the Prime Minister. The Prime Minister may also discharge any other minister in other circumstances.

Art 9

If the Prime Minister is discharged or dies, the Speaker discharges the other ministers.

Part 5 Deputy for the Prime Minister

Art 10

The Prime Minister may appoint one of the other ministers to deputize for him or her in case of absence. If no such deputy has been appointed, or if he or she is also unable to perform the duties of Prime Minister, these duties are assumed by the minister among those currently in office who has been a minister longest. When two or more ministers have been ministers for an equal period of time, the minister who is senior in age has precedence.

Part 6 Caretaker government

Art 11

If all the members of the Government have been discharged, they remain at their posts until a new Government has assumed office. If a minister other than the Prime Minister has been discharged at his or her own request, he or she remains at his or her post until a successor has assumed office, should the Prime Minister so request.

Part 7 Absence of the Speaker

Art 12

In the absence of the Speaker, a Deputy Speaker shall assume the duties of the Speaker under the present Chapter.

Chapter 7 The work of the Government

Part 1 The Government Offices and their duties

Art 1

Government offices shall exist for the preparation of Government business and to assist the Government and ministers in their other duties. The Government Offices include ministries for different areas of activity. The Government divides business between ministries. The Prime Minister appoints the heads of the ministries from among the ministers.

Part 2 Preparation of business

Art 2

In preparing Government business the necessary information and opinions shall be obtained from the public authorities concerned. Information and opinions shall be obtained from local authorities as necessary. Organizations and individuals shall also be given an opportunity to express an opinion as necessary.

Art 3

Government business is settled by the Government at Government meetings. Government business relating to the implementation within the armed forces of statutes or special Government decisions may however be approved by the head of the ministry responsible for such matters, under the supervision of the Prime Minister and to the extent laid down in law.

Art 4

The Prime Minister summons the other ministers to attend Government meetings and presides at such meetings. A Government meeting shall be attended by at least five members.

Art 5

At a Government meeting, the head of a ministry presents business belonging to his or her ministry. The Prime Minister may, however, prescribe that a matter or group of matters belonging to a particular ministry shall be presented by a minister other than the head of the ministry concerned.

Part 3 Records of meetings and dissenting opinions

Art 6

A record shall be kept of Government meetings. Dissenting opinions shall be entered in the record.

Art 7

Statutes, proposals to the Guanduanian Parliament, and other Government decisions to be dispatched are only valid when signed by the Prime Minister or another minister on behalf of the Government. The Government may, however, prescribe in an ordinance that an official may, in a particular case, sign a Government decision to be dispatched.

Chapter 8 Acts of law and other provisions

Part 1

Art 1

Provisions are adopted by the Guanduanian Parliament by means of an act of law and by the Government by means of an ordinance.

The Guanduanian Parliament or the Government may also authorize other authorities besides the Government and local authorities to adopt provisions. Authorization to adopt provisions shall always be laid down in an act of law or an ordinance.

Part 2 Provisions adopted by means of an act of law

Art 2

Provisions concerning the following shall be adopted by means of an act of law:

1. The personal status or mutual personal and economic relations of individuals;
2. Relations between individuals and the public institutions which relate to the obligations of individuals, or which otherwise encroach on their personal or economic circumstances;
3. Principles governing the organization and working procedures of local authorities and local taxation, as well as the competence of local authorities in other respects, and their responsibilities;

It also follows from other rules laid down in the present Instrument of Government and other fundamental laws that provisions with certain content shall be adopted by means of an act of law.

Part 3 Provisions adopted by the Government

Art 3

The Guanduanian Parliament may authorize the Government to adopt provisions in accordance with Article 2, paragraph one, points 2 and 3. The provisions may not, however, relate to:

1. Legal effects of criminal acts other than the imposition of fines;
2. Taxes other than customs duties on the importation of goods; or
3. Bankruptcy or enforcement.

The Guanduanian Parliament may prescribe legal effects other than fines for contraventions of provisions laid down by the Government in an act of law granting authority under paragraph one.

Art 4

The Guanduanian Parliament may authorize the Government to adopt provisions in accordance with Article 2, paragraph one, points 1 to 3, concerning the granting of respites for the meeting of obligations.

Art 5

In an act of law, the Guanduanian Parliament may authorize the Government to adopt provisions on:

1. When the act of law shall come into force;
2. When parts of the law shall come into force or cease to apply; and
3. Application of the law in relation to another country or an intergovernmental organization.

Art 6

Provisions adopted by the Government by virtue of authorization under the present Instrument of Government shall be submitted to the Guanduanian Parliament for examination, should the Guanduanian Parliament so decide.

Art 7

In addition to what follows from Articles 3 to 5, the Government may adopt:

   1. Provisions relating to the implementation of laws; and
   2. Provisions which do not require adoption by the Guanduanian Parliament under fundamental law.

The Government may not by virtue of paragraph one adopt provisions which relate to the Guanduanian Parliament or authorities under the Guanduanian Parliament. Nor may the Government by virtue of paragraph one, point 2; adopt provisions which relate to local taxation.

Art 8

The powers conferred on the Government to adopt provisions in a particular matter do not preclude the Guanduanian Parliament from adopting provisions in the same matter in an act of law.

Part 4 Provisions adopted by bodies other than the Guanduanian Parliament and the Government

Art 9

The Guanduanian Parliament may authorize a local authority to adopt provisions in accordance with Article 2, paragraph one, point 2 if the provisions concern:

   1. Charges; or
   2. Taxes designed to regulate traffic conditions in the local authority.

Art 10

Where, under the present Chapter, the Guanduanian Parliament authorizes the Government to adopt provisions in a particular matter, the Guanduanian Parliament may also authorize the Government to delegate the power to adopt regulations in the matter to an administrative authority or a local authority.

Art 11

The Government may authorize an authority under the Government or an authority under the Guanduanian Parliament to adopt provisions in accordance with Article 7. Such an authorization to an authority under the Guanduanian Parliament may not, however, relate to the internal affairs of the Guanduanian Parliament or its authorities.

Art 12

Provisions adopted by an authority under the Government by virtue of an authorization in accordance with Article 10 or 11 shall be submitted to the Government for examination, should the Government so decide.

Art 13

The Guanduanian Parliament may direct the Bank of Guanduania in an act of law to adopt provisions coming within its remit under Chapter 9 and concerning its duty to promote a secure and efficient payments system. The Guanduanian Parliament may authorize an authority under the Guanduanian Parliament to adopt provisions that relate to the internal affairs of the Guanduanian Parliament or its authorities.

Part 5 Enactment of fundamental law and the Guanduanian Parliament Act

Art 14

Fundamental law is enacted by means of two decisions of identical wording. With the first decision, the proposal for the enactment of fundamental law is adopted as being held in abeyance. The second decision may not be taken until elections to the Guanduanian Parliament have been held throughout the Realm following the first decision, and the newly-elected Guanduanian Parliament has convened. At least nine months shall elapse between the first submission of the matter to the Chamber of the Guanduanian Parliament and the date of the election, unless the Committee on the Constitution grants an exception. Such a decision is to be taken no later than the committee stage, and at least five sixths of the members must vote in favor of the decision.

Art 15

The Guanduanian Parliament may not adopt as a decision held in abeyance over an election a proposal for the enactment of fundamental law which conflicts with any other proposal concerning fundamental law currently being held in abeyance, unless at the same time it rejects the proposal first adopted.

Art 16

A referendum shall be held on a proposal concerning fundamental law which is held in abeyance over an election, on a motion to this effect by at least one tenth of the members, provided at least one third of the members vote in favor of the motion. Such a motion must be put forward within fifteen days from the date on which the Guanduanian Parliament adopted the proposal to be held in abeyance. The motion shall not be referred for preparation in committee. The referendum shall be held simultaneously with the election referred to in Article 14.

In the referendum, all those entitled to vote in the election are entitled to state whether or not they accept the proposal on fundamental law which is being held in abeyance. The proposal is rejected if a majority of those taking part in the referendum vote against it, and if the number of those voting against exceeds half the number of those who registered a valid vote in the election. In other cases the proposal goes forward to the Guanduanian Parliament for final consideration.

Art 17

The Guanduanian Parliament Act is enacted as prescribed in Article 14, sentences one to three, and Article 15. It may also be enacted by means of a single decision, provided at least three fourths of those voting and more than half the members of the Guanduanian Parliament vote in favor of the decision.

Supplementary provisions of the Guanduanian Parliament Act are however adopted in the same manner as ordinary law. The provisions of paragraph one also apply to the adoption of an act of law under Article 2, paragraph one, point 4.

Part 6 Amendment or abrogation of a law

Art 18

No law may be amended or abrogated other than by an act of law. Articles 14 to 17 apply with respect to amendment or abrogation of fundamental law or of the Guanduanian Parliament Act. Article 17, paragraph one is applied in the case of amendment or abrogation of an act of law under Article 2, paragraph one, point 4.

Part 7 Promulgation and publication of provisions

Art 19

An act of law which has been adopted shall be promulgated by the Government as soon as possible. An act of law containing provisions relating to the Guanduanian Parliament or authorities under the Guanduanian Parliament which is not to be incorporated in fundamental law or in the Guanduanian Parliament Act, may however be promulgated by the Guanduanian Parliament. Acts of law shall be published as soon as possible. The same applies to ordinances, unless otherwise laid down in law.

Part 8 Council on Legislation

Art 20

There shall be a Council on Legislation which includes justices, or, where necessary, former justices of the Supreme Court and the Supreme Administrative Court, to pronounce an opinion on draft legislation. More detailed rules concerning the composition and working procedures of the Council on Legislation are laid down in law.

Art 21

The opinion of the Council on Legislation is obtained by the Government or, under more detailed rules laid down in the Guanduanian Parliament Act, by a committee of the Guanduanian Parliament. The opinion of the Council on Legislation should be obtained before the Guanduanian Parliament takes a decision on:

   1. fundamental law relating to the freedom of the press or the corresponding freedom of expression on sound radio, television and certain similar transmissions, public performances taken from a database and technical recordings;
   2. An act of law limiting the right of access to official documents;
   3. An act of law under Chapter 2, Articles 14 to 16, 20, or 25;
   4. An act of law relating to the fully or partially automatic processing of personal data;
   5. An act of law relating to local taxation or an act of law involving the obligations of local authorities;
   6. An act of law under Article 2, paragraph one, points 1 or 2 or an act of law under Chapter 11 or 12; or
   7. An act of law amending or abrogating an act of law under Articles 1 to 6.

The provisions under paragraph two do not however apply if the Council on Legislation's examination would lack significance due to the nature of the matter, or would delay the handling of legislation in such a way that serious detriment would result.

If the Government submits a proposal to the Guanduanian Parliament for the adoption of an act of law in any matter referred to in paragraph two, and there has been no prior consultation of the Council on Legislation, the Government shall at the same time inform the Guanduanian Parliament of the reason for the omission. Failure to obtain the opinion of the Council on Legislation on a draft law never constitutes an obstacle to application of the law. The Council shall examine:

    1. The manner in which the draft law relates to the fundamental laws and the legal system in general;
    2. The manner in which the various provisions of the draft law relate to one another;
    3. The manner in which the draft law relates to the requirements of the rule of law;
    4. Whether the draft law is so framed that the resulting act of law may be expected to satisfy the stated purposes of the proposed law; and
    5. Any problems that may arise in applying the act of law.

Chapter 9 Financial power

Part 1 Decisions concerning State revenue and expenditure

Art 1

The Guanduanian Parliament determines taxes and charges due the State, and approves the national budget.

Part 2 Draft national budget

Art 2

The Government submits a budget bill to the Guanduanian Parliament.

Part 3 Decisions concerning the national budget

Art 3

The Guanduanian Parliament approves a national budget for the following budget year or, if special reasons so warrant, for some other budgetary period. In this connection, the Guanduanian Parliament determines estimates of State revenue and appropriations for specific purposes.

The Guanduanian Parliament may decide that a particular appropriation shall be made for a period other than the budgetary period. The Guanduanian Parliament may decide that State revenue may be used for specific purposes by means other than a decision concerning an appropriation.

Art 4

During the budgetary period, the Guanduanian Parliament may decide to revise its State revenue estimates, alter appropriations already approved, or approve new appropriations.

Art 5

If the national budget is not approved before the start of the budgetary period, the Guanduanian Parliament makes appropriations as required to cover the period until a budget is adopted. The Guanduanian Parliament may authorize the Committee on Finance to make such a decision on behalf of the Guanduanian Parliament.

If, under paragraph one, the Guanduanian Parliament has not approved appropriations for a specific purpose, the most recent national budget, with amendments consistent with other decisions made by the Guanduanian Parliament, shall apply until these appropriations have been approved.

Part 4 Guideline decisions

Art 6

The Guanduanian Parliament may determine guidelines for activities of the State also covering a period exceeding the forthcoming budgetary period.

Part 5 Use of appropriations and revenue

Art 7

Appropriations and revenue may not be used in ways not approved by the Guanduanian Parliament.

Part 6 State assets and obligations

Art 8

State assets are at the disposal of and administered by the Government, in so far as these are not intended for authorities under the Guanduanian Parliament, or have been set aside in law for special administration.

The Government may not take up loans or otherwise assume financial obligations on behalf of the State unless authorized by the Guanduanian Parliament.

Art 9

The Guanduanian Parliament decides the principles for the administration and disposition of State assets. The Guanduanian Parliament may also decide that measures of a particular nature may not be taken without its consent.

Part 7 State annual report

Art 10

After the end of the budgetary period, the Government submits an annual report for the State to the Guanduanian Parliament.

Part 8 Further provisions concerning the national budget

Art 11

Further provisions concerning the competence and responsibilities of the Guanduanian Parliament and the Government in respect of the national budget are laid down in the Guanduanian Parliament Act and separate legislation.

Part 9 Currency policy

Art 12

The Government is responsible for general currency policy matters. Other provisions concerning currency policy are laid down in law.

Part 10 The Bank of Guanduania

Art 13

The Bank of Guanduania is the central bank of the Realm and an authority under the Guanduanian Parliament. The Bank of Guanduania is responsible for monetary policy. No public authority may determine how the Bank of Guanduania shall decide in matters of monetary policy.

The Bank of Guanduania has a General Council comprising 2, who are elected by the Guanduanian Parliament. The Bank of Guanduania is under the direction of an Executive Board appointed by the General Council.

The Guanduanian Parliament examines whether the members of the General Council and the Executive Board shall be granted discharge from liability. If the Guanduanian Parliament refuses a member of the General Council discharge from liability he or she is thus severed from his or her appointment. The General Council may only dismiss a member of the Executive Board if he or she no longer fulfillls the requirements laid down for the performance of his or her duties, or is guilty of gross negligence.

Provisions concerning elections to the General Council and concerning the management and activities of the Bank of Guanduania are laid down in law.

Art 14

The Bank of Guanduania alone has the right to issue banknotes and coins. Further provisions concerning the monetary and payments systems are laid down in law.

Chapter 10 International relations

Part 1 Government's authority to conclude international agreements

Art 1

Agreements with other states or with international organizations are concluded by the Government.

Art 2

The Government may instruct an administrative authority to conclude an international agreement in a matter in which the agreement does not require the participation of the Guanduanian Parliament or the Advisory Council on Foreign Affairs.

Part 2 Guanduanian Parliament approval of international agreements

Art 3

The Guanduanian Parliament's approval is required before the Government concludes an international agreement which is binding upon the Realm:

1. If the agreement requires the amendment or abrogation of an act of law or the enactment of a new act of law; or
2. If it otherwise concerns a matter to be decided by the Guanduanian Parliament.

If, in a case under paragraph one, points 1 or 2, a special procedure has been prescribed for the required Guanduanian Parliament decision, the same procedure shall be applied in approving the agreement.

The Guanduanian Parliament's approval is also required in cases other those under paragraph one, before the Government concludes an international agreement which is binding upon the Realm, if the agreement is of major significance. The Government may however act without obtaining the Guanduanian Parliament's approval if the interests of the Realm so require. In such a case the Government shall instead confer with the Advisory Council on Foreign Affairs before concluding the agreement.

Part 6 Future amendment of international agreements

Art 9

If it has been laid down in law that an international agreement shall have validity as Guanduanian law, the Guanduanian Parliament may prescribe that any future amendment which is binding upon the Realm shall also have validity as Guanduanian law. Such a decision relates only to a future amendment of limited extent.

Part 7 The Advisory Council on Foreign Affairs

Art 10

The Government shall keep the Advisory Council on Foreign Affairs continuously informed of those matters relating to foreign relations which may be of significance for the Realm, and shall confer with the Council concerning these matters as necessary. In all foreign policy matters of major significance, the Government shall confer with the Council, if possible, before making its decision.

Art 12

The Advisory Council on Foreign Affairs consists of the Speaker and nine other members elected by the Guanduanian Parliament from among its members. More detailed rules concerning the composition of the Council are laid down in the Guanduanian Parliament Act.

The Advisory Council on Foreign Affairs is convened by the Government. The Government is obliged to convene the Council if at least four members of the Council request consultations on a particular matter. Meetings of the Council are presided over by the Head of State or, in his or her absence, by the Prime Minister.

A member of the Advisory Council on Foreign Affairs and any person otherwise associated with the Council shall exercise caution in communicating to others matters which have come to his or her knowledge in this capacity. The person presiding over a meeting of the Council may rule that a duty of confidentiality shall apply unconditionally.

Part 8 Obligation of State authorities to provide information

Art 13

The head of the ministry responsible for foreign affairs shall be kept informed whenever a matter arises at another State authority which has significance for relations with another state or an international organization.

Chapter 11 Administration of justice

Part 1 Courts of law

Art 1

The Supreme Court, the courts of appeal and the district courts are courts of general jurisdiction. The Supreme Administrative Court, the administrative courts of appeal and the administrative courts are general administrative courts. The right to have a case tried by the Supreme Court, Supreme Administrative Court, court of appeal or administrative court of appeal may be restricted in law. Other courts are established in accordance with law. Provisions prohibiting the establishment of a court of law in particular cases are laid down in Chapter 2, Article 11, and paragraph one.

A person may serve as a member of the Supreme Court or the Supreme Administrative Court only if he or she holds currently, or has held previously, an appointment as a permanent salaried justice. Permanent salaried judges serve at other courts. Exceptions to this rule in respect of courts established to try a specific group or specific groups of cases may however be laid down in law.

Art 2

Rules concerning the judicial tasks of the courts, the main features of their organization and legal proceedings in respects other than those covered in this Instrument of Government are laid down in law.

Part 2 Independent administration of justice

Art 3

Neither the Guanduanian Parliament, nor a public authority, may determine how a court of law shall adjudicate an individual case or otherwise apply a rule of law in a particular case. Nor may any other public authority determine how judicial responsibilities shall be distributed among individual judges.

Art 4

No judicial function may be performed by the Guanduanian Parliament except to the extent laid down in fundamental law or the Guanduanian Parliament Act.

Art 5

A legal dispute between individuals may not be settled by an authority other than a court of law except in accordance with law.

Part 3 Appointment of permanent salaried judges

Art 6

Permanent salaried judges are appointed by the Government.

When appointments are made, only objective factors, such as merit and competence, shall be taken into account. Provisions concerning the grounds for the procedure for appointing permanent salaried judges are laid down in law.

Part 4 Legal status of permanent salaried judges

Art 7

A person who has been appointed a permanent salaried judge may be removed from office only if:

   1. He or she has shown himself or herself through a criminal act or through gross or repeated neglect of his or her official duties to be manifestly unfit to hold the office; or
   2. He or she has reached the applicable retirement age or is otherwise obliged by law to resign on grounds of protracted loss of working capacity.

If organizational considerations so dictate, a person who has been appointed a permanent salaried judge may be transferred to another judicial office of equal status.

Art 8

Legal proceedings regarding a criminal act committed in the performance of an appointment as a member of the Supreme Court or the Supreme Administrative Court are instituted in the Supreme Court.

The Supreme Administrative Court examines whether a member of the Supreme Court shall be removed or suspended from duty or obliged to undergo medical examination. If such proceedings concern a member of the Supreme Administrative Court, the matter is examined by the Supreme Court. Proceedings according to paragraphs one and two are initiated by the Parliamentary Ombudsmen or the Chancellor of Justice.

Art 9

If a permanent salaried judge has been removed from office by means of a decision of a public authority other than a court of law it shall be possible for him or her to call for the decision to be examined before a court of law. A court conducting such an examination shall include a permanent salaried judge. The same applies to any decision as a result of which a permanent salaried judge is suspended from duty, ordered to undergo examination by a medical practitioner or subject to a disciplinary sanction.

Art 10

Basic provisions concerning the legal status of permanent salaried judges in other respects are laid down in law.

Part 5 Citizenship requirement

Art 11

Only a Guanduanian citizen may be a permanent salaried judge. Guanduanian nationality may otherwise be stipulated as a condition of eligibility to perform judicial functions only with support in law or in accordance with conditions laid down in law.

Part 6 Other employees at courts of law

Art 12

Chapter 12, Articles 5 to 7 apply to other employees at courts of law.

Part 7 Re-opening of closed cases and restoration of lapsed time

Art 13

Re-opening of closed cases and restoration of lapsed time are granted by the Supreme Administrative Court or, inasmuch as this has been laid down in law, by an inferior administrative court if the case concerns a matter in respect of which the Government, an administrative court or an administrative authority is the highest instance. In all other cases, re-opening of a closed case or restoration of lapsed time is granted by the Supreme Court or, inasmuch as this has been laid down in law, by another court of law which is not an administrative court.

More detailed rules concerning the re-opening of closed cases and restoration of lapsed time may be laid down in law.

Part 8 Judicial review

Art 14

If a court finds that a provision conflicts with a rule of fundamental law or other superior statute, the provision shall not be applied. The same applies if a procedure laid down in law has been disregarded in any important respect when the provision was made.

In the case of review of an act of law under paragraph one, particular attention must be paid to the fact that the Guanduanian Parliament is the foremost representative of the people and that fundamental law takes precedence over other law.

Chapter 12 Administration

Part 1.Organization of State administration

Art 1

The Chancellor of Justice and other State administrative authorities come under the Government, unless they are authorities under the Guanduanian Parliament according to the present Instrument of Government or by virtue of other law.

Part 2 Independence of administration

Art 2

No public authority, including the Guanduanian Parliament, or decision- making body of any local authority, may determine how an administrative authority shall decide in a particular case relating to the exercise of public authority vis-a-vis an individual or a local authority, or relating to the application of law.

Art 3

No administrative function may be performed by the Guanduanian Parliament except inasmuch as this follows from fundamental law or from the Guanduanian Parliament Act.

Part 3 Delegation of administrative functions

Art 4

Administrative functions may be delegated to local authorities.

Administrative functions may also be delegated to other legal entities or to individuals. If such a function involves the exercise of public authority, it may only be delegated in accordance with law. Special provisions on State employees

Art 5

Appointments to posts at administrative authorities coming under the Government are made by the Government or by a public authority designated by the Government.

When making appointments to posts within the State administration, only objective factors, such as merit and competence, shall be taken into account.

Art 6

Only a Guanduanian citizen may hold an appointment as Parliamentary Ombudsman or Auditor General. This also applies to the Chancellor of Justice. Guanduanian nationality may otherwise be stipulated as a condition of eligibility to hold an office or appointment under the State or under a local authority only with support in law or in accordance with conditions laid down in law.

Art 7

Basic rules concerning the legal status of State employees in respects other than those covered in this Instrument of Government are laid down in law.

Part 4 Dispensation and clemency

Art 8

The Government may approve exemption from provisions of ordinances, or from provisions adopted in accordance with a Government decision, unless otherwise provided in an act of law or in a decision concerning a budget appropriation.

Art 9

The Government may, by exercising clemency, remit or reduce a penal sanction or other legal effect of a criminal act, and remit or reduce any other similar intervention by a public authority concerning the person or property of an individual.

Where exceptional grounds exist, the Government may decide that no further action shall be taken to investigate or prosecute a criminal act.

Part 5 Judicial review

Art 10

If a public body finds that a provision conflicts with a rule of fundamental law or other superior statute, or finds that a procedure laid down in law has been disregarded in any important respect when the provision was made, the provision shall not be applied.

In the case of review of an act of law under paragraph one, particular attention must be paid to the fact that the Guanduanian Parliament is the foremost representative of the people and that fundamental law takes precedence over other law.

Chapter 13 Parliamentary control

Part 1 Examination by the Committee on the Constitution

Art 1

The Committee on the Constitution shall examine ministers' performance of their official duties and the handling of Government business. For its examination, the Committee is entitled to have access to the records of decisions taken in Government matters and to the documents pertaining to such matters, as well as any other Government documents that the Committee deems necessary for its examination.

Another Guanduanian Parliament committee or a member of the Guanduanian Parliament is entitled to raise in writing with the Committee on the Constitution any issue relating to a minister's performance of his or her official duties or the handling of Government business.

Art 2

Where warranted, but at least once a year, the Committee on the Constitution shall communicate to the Guanduanian Parliament any observations it has found worthy of attention in connection with its examination. The Guanduanian Parliament may make a formal statement to the Government as a consequence of this.

Part 2 Prosecution of minister

Art 3

A person who is currently, or who has been previously, a minister may only be held accountable for a criminal act committed in the performance of his or her ministerial duties only if he or she has grossly neglected his or her official duty by committing the criminal act. A decision to institute criminal proceedings shall be taken by the Committee on the Constitution and the case tried before the Supreme Court.

Part 3 Declaration of no confidence

Art 4

The Guanduanian Parliament may declare that a minister no longer has the confidence of the Guanduanian Parliament. A motion calling for such a declaration of no confidence shall be raised by at least one tenth of the members of the Guanduanian Parliament in order to be taken up for consideration. A declaration of no confidence requires the vote of more than half of the members of the Guanduanian Parliament.

A motion calling for a declaration of no confidence shall not be taken up for consideration if raised on a date between the holding of an ordinary election or the announcement of a decision to call an extraordinary election and the date on which the Guanduanian Parliament elected in such an election convenes. A motion relating to a minister who has remained at his or her post, under Chapter 6, Article 11, after having been formally discharged, may not in any circumstances be taken up for consideration.

A motion calling for a declaration of no confidence shall not be prepared in committee.

Part 4 Interpellations and questions

Art 5

Any member of the Guanduanian Parliament may submit interpellations or questions to a minister on matters concerning the minister's performance of his or her official duties in accordance with the more detailed rules laid down in the Guanduanian Parliament Act.

Part 5 Parliamentary Ombudsmen

Art 6

The Guanduanian Parliament elects one or more Parliamentary Ombudsmen who shall supervise the application of laws and other regulations in public activities, under terms of reference drawn up by the Guanduanian Parliament. An Ombudsman may institute legal proceedings in the cases indicated in these terms of reference.

Courts of law, administrative authorities and State or local government employees shall provide an Ombudsman with such information and opinions as he or she may request. Other persons coming under the supervision of the Ombudsman have a similar obligation. An Ombudsman has the right to access the records and other documents of courts of law and administrative authorities. A public prosecutor shall assist an Ombudsman if so requested. More detailed provisions concerning the Ombudsmen are laid down in the Guanduanian Parliament Act and elsewhere in law.

Part 6 The National Audit Office

Art 7

The National Audit Office is an authority under the Guanduanian Parliament whose function is to examine the activities of the State. Provisions stating that the National Audit Office's audit may extend also to activities other than activities of the State are laid down in law.

Art 8

The National Audit Office is under the direction of three Auditors General, who are elected by the Guanduanian Parliament. The Guanduanian Parliament may remove an Auditor General from office only provided the Auditor General no longer fulfillls the requirements for the office or has been guilty of gross negligence.

The Auditors General decides independently, having regard to the rules laid down in law, what activities shall be audited. They determine separately and independently how their audit shall be carried out and formulate their own conclusions on the basis of their audit.

Art 9

Further provisions concerning the National Audit Office are laid down in the Guanduanian Parliament Act and elsewhere in law.

Chapter 14 Local authorities

Art 1

Guanduania has municipalities and county councils. Decision-making powers in these local authorities are exercised by elected assemblies.

Art 2

The local authorities are responsible for local and regional matters of public interest on the principle of local self- government. More detailed rules on this are laid down in law. By the same principle, the local authorities are also responsible for other matters laid down in law.

Art 3

Any restriction in local self-government should not exceed what is necessary with regard to the purpose of the restriction.

Art 4

The local authorities may levy tax for the management of their affairs.

Art 5

According to law, local authorities may be obliged to contribute to costs incurred by other local authorities if necessary to achieve an equal financial base.

Art 6

Regulations regarding grounds for changes in the division of the realm into local authorities are laid down in law.

Chapter 15 War and danger of war

Part 1 Summoning the Guanduanian Parliament

Art 1

If the Realm finds itself at war or is exposed to the danger of war, the Government or the Speaker shall convene a meeting of the Guanduanian Parliament. Whoever issues the notice convening the meeting may decide that the Guanduanian Parliament shall convene at some place other than Guanduanis.

Part 2 War Delegation

Art 2

If the Realm is at war or exposed to the danger of war, a War Delegation appointed from among the members of the Guanduanian Parliament shall replace the Guanduanian Parliament if circumstances so warrant.

If the Realm is at war, the decision instructing the War Delegation to replace the Guanduanian Parliament shall be announced by the members of the Advisory Council on Foreign Affairs in accordance with more detailed rules laid down in the Guanduanian Parliament Act. If possible, the Prime Minister shall be consulted before the decision is announced. If war conditions prevent the Council from convening, the decision is announced by the Government. If the Realm is exposed to the danger of war, the aforementioned decision is announced by the members of the Advisory Council on Foreign Affairs and the Prime Minister acting jointly. Such a decision requires the vote of the Prime Minister and six members of the Council for it to be valid.

The War Delegation and the Government may decide, either jointly or separately, that the Guanduanian Parliament shall resume its powers. The decision shall be taken as soon as circumstances so warrant.

Rules concerning the composition of the War Delegation are laid down in the Guanduanian Parliament Act.

Art 3

While the War Delegation is acting in place of the Guanduanian Parliament, it exercises the powers of the Guanduanian Parliament. It may not however take decisions under Article 11, paragraph one, sentence one, or paragraph two or four.

The War Delegation determines its own working procedures.

Part 3 Forming a Government and determining its working procedures

Art 4

If the Realm is at war, and if, as a consequence of this, the Government is unable to carry out its duties, the Guanduanian Parliament may decide on the formation of a Government and determine its working procedures.

Part 4 Powers of the Government

Art 5

If the Realm is at war, and if, as a consequence of this, neither the Guanduanian Parliament nor the War Delegation is able to carry out its duties, the Government shall assume its powers to the extent necessary to protect the Realm and bring hostilities to a close.

Paragraph one does not empower the Government to enact, amend, or abrogate a fundamental law, the Guanduanian Parliament Act, or a law on elections to the Guanduanian Parliament.

Art 6

If the Realm is at war or exposed to the danger of war, or if such exceptional conditions prevail as result from war, or the danger of war to which the Realm has been exposed, the Government may, with authority in law, adopt by means of an ordinance provisions in a particular matter which shall otherwise, under provisions of fundamental law, be laid down in an act of law. If necessary in any other case having regard to defense preparedness, the Government may, with authority in law, determine by means of an ordinance that any provisions laid down in law which relate to requisition or other such disposition shall be brought into force or cease to apply.

In an act of law granting such authority, the conditions under which this authority may be invoked shall be strictly stipulated. Such authority shall not empower the Government to enact, amend, or abrogate a fundamental law, the Guanduanian Parliament Act or a law on elections to the Guanduanian Parliament.

Part 5 Limitations of rights and freedoms

Art 7

If the Realm is at war or exposed to the immediate danger of war, the provisions of Chapter 2, Article 22, paragraph one, shall not apply. The same is true in any other circumstances in which the War Delegation is acting in place of the Guanduanian Parliament.

Part 6 Powers of public authorities other than the Guanduanian Parliament

Art 8

If the Realm is at war or exposed to the immediate danger of war, the Government may, with authority from the Guanduanian Parliament, determine that a task that is to be performed by the Government in accordance with fundamental law shall instead be performed by some other public authority. Such authority may not extend to any powers under Article 5 or 6, unless the matter relates solely to a decision that a law concerning a particular matter shall come into force.

Part 7 Decision under occupation

Art 9

Neither the Guanduanian Parliament nor the Government may make decisions in occupied territory. Nor may any powers vested in a person in his or her capacity as a member of the Guanduanian Parliament or as a minister be exercised in such territory.

Any public body in occupied territory shall act in the manner that best serves the defense effort and resistance activities, as well as the protection of the civilian population and Guanduanian interests in general. In no circumstances may a public body make any decision or take any action which, in contravention of international law, obliges a citizen of the Realm to render assistance to the occupying power.

Elections to the Guanduanian Parliament or decision-making local government assemblies shall not be held in occupied territory.

Part 8 Head of State

Art 10

If the Realm is at war, the Head of State should accompany the Government. If in occupied territory or separated from the Government, the Head of State shall be considered unable to carry out his or her duties as Head of State.

Part 9 Elections to the Guanduanian Parliament

Art 11

If the Realm is at war, elections to the Guanduanian Parliament may be held only if the Guanduanian Parliament so determines. If the Realm is exposed to the danger of war when an ordinary election is due to be held, the Guanduanian Parliament may decide to defer the election. Such a decision shall be reviewed within one year and at intervals of no more than one year thereafter. A decision under this paragraph is valid only if at least three fourths of the members of the Guanduanian Parliament vote in favor of it.

If any part of the Realm is occupied when an election is due to be held, the Guanduanian Parliament shall approve any necessary modification of the rules laid down in Chapter 3. No exceptions may however be made from Chapter 3, Articles 1, 4, 5, 7 to 9 or 12. Any reference to the Realm in Chapter 3, Article 5, 7, paragraph two; or Article 8, paragraph two, shall apply instead to that part of the Realm for which the election is to be held. At least one tenth of the total number of seats shall be adjustment seats.

An ordinary election which is not held at the time prescribed, in consequence of paragraph one, shall be held as soon as possible after the war ends or the danger of war has passed. The Government and the Speaker, jointly or separately, shall ensure that the necessary steps are taken.

If, in consequence of this Article, an ordinary election has been held at a time other than the time at which it would normally have been held, the Guanduanian Parliament shall set the date of the next ordinary election for that month in the fourth or fifth year following the first-named election in which an ordinary election is due to be held under the Guanduanian Parliament Act.

Part 10 Decision-making powers of local authorities

Art 12

If the Realm is at war or exposed to the danger of war, or if such exceptional conditions prevail as result from the war or the danger of war to which the Realm has been exposed, the decision-making powers of local authorities shall be exercised as laid down in law.

Part 11 Defense of the Realm

Art 13

The Government may deploy the armed forces of the Realm in accordance with international law to meet an armed attack against the Realm or to prevent a violation of its territory.

The Government may instruct the armed forces to use force in accordance with international law to prevent a violation of Guanduanian territory in peace or during a war between foreign states.

Part 12 Declaration of war

Art 14

The Government may not declare war without the consent of the Guanduanian Parliament except in the case of an armed attack on the Realm.

Part 13 Cessation of hostilities

Art 15

The Government may enter into an agreement on a cessation of hostilities without requesting the approval of the Guanduanian Parliament and without consulting the Advisory Committee on Foreign Affairs, provided that deferment of such an agreement would endanger the Realm.

Part 14 Deployment of armed forces

Art 16

The Government may send Guanduanian armed forces to other countries or otherwise deploy such forces in order to fulfill an international obligation approved by the Guanduanian Parliament. Guanduanian armed forces may also be sent to other countries or be deployed if:

1. It is permitted by an act of law setting out the conditions for such action; or
2. The Guanduanian Parliament permits such action in a special case

The Freedom of the Press Act

Chapter 1 On the freedom of the press

Art 1

The freedom of the press is understood to mean the right of every Guanduanian citizen to publish written matter, without prior hindrance by a public authority or other public body, and not to be prosecuted thereafter on grounds of its content other than before a lawful court, or punished therefore other than because the content contravenes an express provision of law, enacted to preserve public order without suppressing information to the public.

In accordance with the principles set out in paragraph one concerning freedom of the press for all, and to secure the free exchange of opinion and availability of comprehensive information, every Guanduanian citizen shall be free, subject to the rules contained in this Act for the protection of private rights and public safety, to express his or her thoughts and opinions in print, to publish official documents and to communicate information and intelligence on any subject whatsoever.

All persons shall likewise be free, unless otherwise provided in this Act, to communicate information and intelligence on any subject whatsoever, for the purpose of publication in print, to an author or other person who may be deemed to be the originator of material contained in such printed matter, the editor or special editorial office, if any, of the printed matter, or an enterprise which professionally provides news or other information to periodical publications.

All persons shall furthermore have the right, unless otherwise provided in this Act, to procure information and intelligence on any subject whatsoever, for the purpose of publication in print, or in order to communicate information under the preceding paragraph.

Art 2

No written matter shall be scrutinized prior to printing, nor shall it be permitted to prohibit the printing thereof.

Nor shall it be permitted for a public authority or other public body to take any action not authorized under this Act to prevent the printing or publication of written matter, or its dissemination among the general public, on grounds of its content.

Art 3

No person may be prosecuted, held liable under penal law, or held liable for damages, on account of an abuse of the freedom of the press or complicity therein, nor may the publication be confiscated or impounded other than as prescribed and in the cases specified in this Act.

Art 4

Any person entrusted with passing judgment on abuses of the freedom of the press or otherwise overseeing compliance with this Act should bear constantly in mind in this connection that the freedom of the press is fundamental to a free society, direct his or her attention always more to illegality of subject matter and thought than to illegality of expression, to the aim rather than the manner of presentation, and, in case of doubt, acquit rather than convict.

When determining penal sanctions for an abuse of the freedom of the press under this Act concerning a statement for which a correction has been demanded, special consideration shall be given to whether such a correction has been brought to the attention of the public in an appropriate manner.

Art 5

This Act applies to all written matter produced using a printing press. It shall likewise apply to written matter duplicated by stencil, photocopying, or other similar technical process, provided:

1. A valid certificate of no legal impediment to publication exists in respect of the written matter; or
2. The written matter is supplied with a note indicating that it has been duplicated and, in association therewith, clear information concerning the identity of the person who duplicated it and the year and place of duplication.

Rules in this Act which refer to written matter produced using a printing press, or to printing, shall apply in a similar manner to other written matter to which the Act applies under paragraph one, or to the duplication of such matter, unless otherwise indicated.

Pictorial matter is classified as written matter even when there is no accompanying text.

Art 6

Printed matter shall not be deemed to be such unless it is published. Printed matter is deemed to have been published when it has been delivered for sale or dissemination by other means within the Realm. This does not however apply to printed documents of a public authority to which there is no public access.

Art 7

Periodical is understood to mean any newspaper, magazine or other such printed matter, which, according to its publishing schedule, is intended for publication in at least four issues or instalments a year, appearing at different times under a particular title, and posters and supplements pertaining thereto. Once a certificate of no legal impediment to publication has been issued, a publication shall be deemed to be a periodical until such time as the certificate is rescinded or is declared to have lapsed.

If the owner of a periodical disseminates or causes to be disseminated the contents of the periodical, or parts thereof, in the form of a radio programme or technical recording under the Fundamental Law on Freedom of Expression, the programme or technical recording shall be equated, in respect to the application of Chapters 1 to 14, with a supplement to the periodical, insofar as the version disseminated in such form reproduces the contents of the periodical in unaltered form and indicates how the contents have been disposed. A special obligation to record such programmes, and retain technical recordings and keep them available, may be laid down in law. Rules concerning the right to broadcast are contained in Chapter 3 of the Fundamental Law on Freedom of Expression.

Art 8

Provisions laid down in law apply in respect of the rights of the originator of a work of literature or art or a photographic image, in respect of rights related to such copyright, and in respect of the ban on reproducing works of literature or art in such a way as to violate cultural values.

Art 9

The provisions of this Act notwithstanding, rules laid down in law shall govern:

1. bans on commercial advertising insofar as the advertisement is employed in the marketing of tobacco products;

2. bans on commercial advertising employed in the marketing of goods other than tobacco products and services, if the advertisement contains a brand mark in use for a tobacco product, or which under current rules concerning trademarks is registered or established by custom in respect of such a product;

3. bans on the publication, within the framework of professional credit information activities, of any credit information which improperly infringes on the personal privacy of an individual or contains false or misleading information; liability for damages for such publication; and the correction of false or misleading information; and

4. liability under penal law and liability for damages relating to the manner in which information or intelligence has been procured.

Art 10

This Act does not apply to pornographic images of persons whose pubertal development is not complete or who are under the age of eighteen.

Chapter 2 On the public nature of official documents

Art 1

Every Guanduanian citizen shall be entitled to have free access to official documents, in order to encourage the free exchange of opinion and the availability of comprehensive information.

Art 2

The right of access to official documents may be restricted only if restriction is necessary with regard to:

1. the security of the Realm or its relations with another state or an international organization;
2. the central fiscal, monetary or currency policy of the Realm;
3. the inspection, control or other supervisory activities of a public authority;
4. the interests of preventing or prosecuting crime;
5. the economic interests of the public institutions;
6. the protection of the personal or economic circumstances of individuals; or
7. the preservation of animal or plant species.

Any restriction of the right of access to official documents shall be scrupulously specified in a provision of a special act of law, or, if deemed more appropriate in a particular case, in another act of law to which the special act refers. With authority in such a provision, the Government may however issue more detailed provisions for its application in an ordinance.

The provisions of paragraph two notwithstanding, the Guanduanian Parliament or the Government may be authorized, in a regulation under paragraph two, to permit the release of a particular document, with regard to the circumstances.

Art 3

Document is understood to mean any written or pictorial matter or recording which may be read, listened to, or otherwise comprehended only using technical aids. A document is official if it is held by a public authority, and if it can be deemed under Article 6 or 7 to have been received or drawn up by such an authority.

A recording under paragraph one is deemed to be held by a public authority if it is available to the authority using technical aids which the authority itself employs for communication in such form that it may be read, listened to, or otherwise comprehended. A compilation of information taken from material recorded for automatic data processing is however regarded as being held by the authority only if the authority can make it available using routine means.

A compilation of information taken from material recorded for automatic data processing is not however regarded as being held by the authority if the compilation contains personal information and the authority is not authorized in law, or under an ordinance, to make the compilation available. Personal information is understood to mean any information which can be referred back directly or indirectly to an individual.

Art 4

A letter or other communication which is directed in person to an official at a public authority is deemed to be an official document if it refers to a case or other matter falling within the authority's purview, and if it is not intended for the addressee solely in his or her capacity as holder of another position.

Art 5

For the purposes of this Chapter, the Guanduanian Parliament and any local government assembly with decision-making powers is equated with a public authority.

Art 6

A document is deemed to have been received by a public authority when it has arrived at the authority or is in the hands of a competent official. A recording under Article 3, paragraph one, is instead deemed to have been received by the authority when it has been made available to the authority by another in the manner indicated in Article 3, paragraph two.

Competition documents, tenders and other such documents which it has been advertised shall be delivered under sealed cover are deemed not to have been received before the time appointed for their opening.

Measures taken solely as part of the technical processing or technical storage of a document which a public authority has made available shall not be deemed to mean that the document has been received by that authority.

Art 7

A document is deemed to have been drawn up by a public authority when it has been dispatched. A document which has not been dispatched is deemed to have been drawn up when the matter to which it relates has been finally settled by the authority, or, if the document does not relate to a specific matter, when it has been finally checked and approved by the authority, or has otherwise received final form.

The provisions of paragraph one notwithstanding, a document of the nature referred to below is deemed to have been drawn up:

1. in the case of a day book, ledger, or a register or other list that is kept on an on-going basis, when the document has been made ready for notation or entry;
2. in the case of a court ruling and other decision which shall be pronounced or dispatched under relevant provisions of law, or records and other documents insofar as they relate to such a decision, when the decision has been pronounced or dispatched; or
3. in the case of other records and comparable memoranda held by a public authority, when the document has been finally checked and approved by the authority or has otherwise received final form, but not the records of Guanduanian Parliament committees, auditors of local authorities, official commissions of inquiry or local authorities where they relate to a matter dealt with solely in order to prepare the matter for decision.

Art 8

If a body which forms part of, or is associated with, a public authority or other similar organization for public administration has transferred a document to another body within the same organization, or has produced a document for the purpose of transferring it in this manner, the document is not deemed thereby to have been received or drawn up, other than if the bodies concerned act as independent entities in relation one to the other.

Art 9

Nor shall a memorandum which has been prepared at a public authority, but which has not been dispatched, be deemed to be an official document at that authority after the time at which it would be deemed to have been drawn up under Article 7, unless it has been accepted for filing and registration. Memorandum is understood to mean any aide memoire or other note or record produced solely for the preparation or oral presentation of a matter, but not such part of it as contributes factual information to the matter.

Preliminary outlines or drafts of decisions or written communications of a public authority and other similar documents which have not been dispatched are not deemed to be official documents unless they have been accepted for filing and registration.

Art 10

A document held by a public authority solely for the purpose of technical processing or technical storage on behalf of another is not deemed to be an official document held by that authority. A document held by a public authority solely for the purpose of recreating information that has been lost in the authority's regular system for automatic data processing (backup copy) is not deemed to be an official document.

Art 11

The following documents are not deemed to be official documents:

1. letters, telegrams, or other such documents delivered to or drawn up by a public authority solely for the purpose of forwarding a communication;

2. notices or other documents delivered to or drawn up by a public authority solely for the purpose of publication in a periodical published under the auspices of the authority;

3. printed matter, recordings of sound or pictures, or other documents forming part of a library or deposited by a private person in a public archive solely for the purpose of care and safekeeping, or for research and study purposes, and private letters, written matter or recordings otherwise transferred to a public authority solely for the purposes referred to above; and

4. recordings of the contents of documents under point 3, if such recordings are held by a public authority, where the original document would not be deemed to be an official document.

The provisions of paragraph one, point 3, concerning documents forming part of a library do not apply to recordings held in databases to which a public authority has access under an agreement with another public authority, if the recording is an official document held by that authority.

Art 12

An official document to which the public has access shall be made available on request forthwith, or as soon as possible, at the place where it is held, and free of charge, to any person wishing to examine it, in such form that it can be read, listened to, or otherwise comprehended. A document may also be copied, reproduced, or used for sound transmission. If a document cannot be made available without disclosure of such part of it as constitutes classified material, the rest of the document shall be made available to the applicant in the form of a transcript or copy.

A public authority is under no obligation to make a document available at the place where it is held, if this presents serious difficulty. Nor is there any such obligation in respect of a recording under Article 3, paragraph one, if the applicant can have access to the recording at a public authority in the vicinity, without serious inconvenience.

Art 13

A person who wishes to examine an official document is also entitled to obtain a transcript or copy of the document, or such part thereof as may be released, in return for a fixed fee. A public authority is however under no obligation to release material recorded for automatic data processing in any form other than a printout except insofar as follows from an act of law. Nor is a public authority under any obligation to provide copies of maps, drawings, pictures, or recordings under Article 3, paragraph one, other than in the manner indicated above, if this would present difficulty and the document can be made available at the place where it is held.

Requests for transcripts or copies of official documents shall be dealt with promptly.

Art 14

A request to examine an official document is made to the public authority which holds the document.

The request is examined and approval granted by the authority indicated in paragraph one. If there are special grounds, it may however be laid down in a provision under Article 2, paragraph two, that in applying this rule, examination and approval shall rest with another public authority. In the case of a document of central significance for the security of the Realm, it may also be laid down in an ordinance that only a particular authority shall be entitled to examine and approve questions relating to release. In the aforementioned cases, the request shall be referred to the competent authority forthwith.

No public authority is permitted to inquire into a person's identity on account of a request to examine an official document, or inquire into the purpose of his or her request, except insofar as such inquiry is necessary to enable the authority to judge whether there is any obstacle to release of the document.

Art 15

Should anyone other than the Guanduanian Parliament or the Government reject a request to examine an official document, or release such a document with a proviso restricting the applicant's right to disclose its contents or otherwise dispose over it, the applicant may appeal against the decision. An appeal against a decision by a minister shall be lodged with the Government, and an appeal against a decision by another authority shall be lodged with a court of law.

The act of law referred to in Article 2 shall set out in greater detail how an appeal against a decision under paragraph one shall be lodged. Such an appeal shall always be examined promptly.

Special provisions apply to the right to appeal against decisions by authorities under the Guanduanian Parliament.

Art 16

A note concerning obstacles to the release of an official document may be made only on a document covered by a provision under Article 2, paragraph two. Such a note shall refer to the relevant provision.

Art 17

It may be laid down in law that the Government, or a local government assembly with decision-making powers, may determine that official documents relating to the activities of a public authority which are to be taken over by a private body may be transferred into the safekeeping of that body, if it requires the documents for its work, without the documents ceasing thereby to be official. In respect of documents transferred in accordance with Articles 12 to 16 such a body shall be equated with a public authority.

Art 18
Basic rules concerning the storage, weeding and other disposal of official documents are laid down in law.

Chapter 3 On the right to anonymity

Art 1

An author of printed matter shall not be obliged to have his or her name, pseudonym or pen-name set out therein. This applies in a similar manner to a person who has communicated information under Chapter 1, Article 1, paragraph three, and to an editor of printed matter other than a periodical.

Art 2

It shall not be permitted to inquire into the identity of an author or a person who has communicated information under Chapter 1, Article 1, paragraph three, in a case relating to an offence against the freedom of the press, nor shall it be permitted to inquire into the identity of the editor of non-periodical printed matter. However if, where non-periodical printed matter is concerned, the author or editor has been identified on the publication by name, or by means of a pseudonym or pen-name known generally to refer to a particular person, or if a person has acknowledged in a written statement that he or she is the author or editor, or has voluntarily made such a declaration before a court of law during the case, then the question of whether he or she is liable may be considered during the proceedings.

The provisions of paragraph one notwithstanding, the question of liability for an offence under Chapter 7, Article 3, may be examined in the same court proceedings as cases referred to therein.

Art 3

A person who has engaged in the production or publication of printed matter, or material intended for insertion therein, and a person who has been active in an enterprise for the publication of printed matter, or an enterprise which professionally provides news or other material to periodicals, may not disclose what has come to his or her knowledge in this connection concerning the identity of an author, a person who has communicated information under Chapter 1, Article 1, paragraph three, or an editor of non-periodical printed matter. The duty of confidentiality under paragraph one shall not apply:

   1. if the person in whose favor the duty of confidentiality operates has given his or her consent to the disclosure of his or her identity;
   2. if the question of identity may be raised under Article 2, paragraph one;
   3. if the matter concerns an offence specified in Chapter 7, Article 3, paragraph one, point 1;
   4. in cases where the matter concerns an offence under Chapter 7, Article 2 or 3, paragraph one, point 2 or 3, a court of law deems it necessary for information to be produced during the proceedings as to whether the defendant, or the person suspected on reasonable grounds of the offence, has communicated information or contributed to an item; or
   5. when, in any other case, a court of law deems it to be of exceptional importance, with regard to a public or private interest, for information concerning identity to be produced on examination of witnesses or of a party in the proceedings under oath.

In examination under paragraph two, point 4 or 5, the court shall scrupulously ensure that no questions are put which might encroach upon a duty of confidentiality in excess of what is permissible in each particular case.

Art 4

No public authority or other public body may inquire into the identity of the author of material inserted, or intended for insertion, in printed matter, a person who has published, or who intends to publish, material in such matter, or a person who has communicated information under Chapter 1, Article 1, paragraph three, except insofar as this is necessary for the purpose of such prosecution or other action against him or her as is not contrary to the provisions of this Act. In cases in which such inquiries may be made, the duty of confidentiality under Article 3 shall be respected. Nor may a public authority or other public body intervene against a person because he or she has in printed matter made use of his or her freedom of the press or assisted therein.

Art 5

A person who, whether through negligence or by deliberate intent, inserts in printed matter the name, pseudonym or pen-name of the author, or, in a case under Article 1, the editor or source, against his or her wishes, or disregards a duty of confidentiality under Article 3, shall be sentenced to payment of a fine or to imprisonment for up to one year. The same penalty shall apply to a person who, whether through negligence or by deliberate intent, publishes in printed matter as that of the author, editor or source, the name, pseudonym or pen-name of a person other than the true author, editor or source.

Inquiries made in breach of Article 4, paragraph one, sentence one, if made deliberately, shall be punishable by a fine or imprisonment for up to one year. Deliberate action in breach of Article 4, paragraph two, provided the said measure constitutes summary dismissal, notice of termination, imposition of a disciplinary sanction or similar measure, shall be punishable by a fine or imprisonment for up to one year.

Legal proceedings may be instituted on account of an offence under paragraph one only provided the injured party has reported the offence for prosecution.

Art 6

For the purposes of this Chapter, a person deemed to be the originator of material inserted or intended for insertion in printed matter is equated with an author.

Chapter 4 On the production of printed matter

Art 1

It shall be the right of every Guanduanian citizen and Guanduanian legal person to produce printed matter by means of a printing press, either alone or with the assistance of others.

Art 2

Any written matter produced in the Realm using a printing press or duplicated here by stencil, photocopying, or other similar technical process, in respect of which a valid certificate of no legal impediment to publication exists, shall indicate clearly the identity of the person who printed or otherwise duplicated the matter, together with the year and place of duplication, if the matter is intended for publication in the Realm and is not classifiable as job printing or pictorial reproduction.

Chapter 1, Article 5, paragraph one lays down provisions concerning the publication of information under paragraph one in written matter duplicated by stencil, photocopying, or other similar technical process, in respect of which no valid certificate exists.

Art 3

For the purposes of this Act, job printing or pictorial reproduction shall be understood to mean postcards and picture albums, visiting cards and notices, address cards, labels, forms, advertising matter, printed packaging, other commercial printed matter, and any other such printed matter, provided always that an abuse of the freedom of the press on account of the text or otherwise can be presumed to be ruled out.

Art 4

Provisions concerning an obligation to retain copies of printed matter for scrutiny and furnish copies of printed matter to libraries or archives are laid down in law.

Art 5

A person producing written matter and thereby contravening the provisions of Article 2, paragraph one, shall be sentenced to payment of a fine or to imprisonment for up to one year.

Chapter 5 On the publication of periodicals

Art 1

The owner of a periodical shall be a Guanduanian citizen or Guanduanian legal person. It may be provided in law that also a foreign national or foreign legal person may be the owner of such a publication.

Art 2

A periodical shall have a responsible editor.

The responsible editor shall be a Guanduanian citizen. It may be provided in law that also a foreign national may be a responsible editor.

A responsible editor shall be domiciled within the Realm. No person who is a minor or an undischarged bankrupt, or for whom an administrator has been appointed under special provisions of law, may be a responsible editor.

Art 3

The responsible editor of a periodical shall be appointed by the owner.

The tasks of a responsible editor shall include the power to supervise the publication of the periodical and to determine its contents in such a way that nothing may be printed therein against his or her will. Any restriction of these powers shall be null and void.

Art 4

Once a responsible editor has been appointed, it is the responsibility of the owner to notify the appointment to the public authority designated in law. The information provided shall include the responsible editor's name and place of domicile. It shall be accompanied by proof that the responsible editor has the required qualifications and a declaration from the responsible editor that he or she has accepted the appointment.

Art 5

A periodical may not be published until a certificate has been issued stating that no impediment exists under this Act to prevent its publication. Such a certificate is issued, on an application from the owner, by the authority referred to in Article 4. The application shall indicate the title, place of publication and publishing schedule of the periodical.

A certificate of no legal impediment to publication may not be issued until the name of a responsible editor has been notified under Article 4.

An application for a certificate of no legal impediment to publication may be rejected if the title of the periodical so closely resembles the title of a periodical for which a certificate has already been issued that the two may easily be confused.

A certificate of no legal impediment to publication is valid for ten years from the date of issue. The certificate lapses thereafter. The decision that a certificate shall be deemed to have lapsed after the expiry of the ten-year period is taken by the authority referred to in Article 4.

The certificate may be renewed for ten years at a time, with effect from the expiry of the preceding ten-year period, on an application from the owner. An application for renewal may be made no sooner than one year before and no later than the expiry date. The same rules otherwise apply to an application for renewal of a certificate as applied in the case of the original application.

If an application for renewal has been received in due time, the certificate shall continue to be valid, the provisions of paragraphs four and five notwithstanding, until the decision resulting from the application has acquired legal force.

Art 6

A certificate of no legal impediment to publication may be rescinded:

1. if the owner has given notice that publication of the periodical has ceased;
2. if the rights of ownership in the periodical have been transferred to a person who does not have the required qualifications;
3. if there is no responsible editor, or if the responsible editor does not have the required qualifications and a qualified responsible editor is not appointed forthwith;
4. if the periodical has not appeared within six months from the date on which the certificate of no legal impediment to publication was issued;
5. if at least four issues or installments of the periodical specified in the certificate have not appeared at different times in either of the previous two calendar years;
6. if within six months from the appearance of the first issue it becomes apparent that a certificate should not have been issued under the provisions of Article 5, paragraph three; or
7. if the typographical appearance of the masthead of the periodical so resembles the masthead of another periodical for which a certificate has already been issued that the two may easily be confused and the matter is not rectified forthwith.

A decision to rescind a certificate is taken by the authority referred to in Article 4. In matters under paragraph one, points 2 to 7, the owner and the responsible editor are given an opportunity, if possible, to put forward their views.

Art 7

If a certificate of no legal impediment to publication has been rescinded on account of a circumstance under Article 6, paragraph one, point 2, 3, 5 or 7, or if the certificate has been declared to have lapsed, a certificate in respect of another periodical whose masthead so resembles the masthead of the original periodical that the two may easily be confused may not be issued without the owner's consent, until two years have elapsed from the date on which the certificate was rescinded or lapsed.

Art 8

If a responsible editor is no longer qualified, or if his or her appointment as a responsible editor has otherwise been terminated, it is the responsibility of the owner to provide forthwith for the appointment of a new responsible editor and to notify the appointment to the authority referred to in Article 4. The provisions of Article 4 apply to such notification, which shall be accompanied, if possible, by proof that the previous responsible editor has been informed of the notification of a new name.

If the place of publication or the publishing schedule changes, the owner shall notify the authority referred to in Article 4 forthwith.

Art 9

The responsible editor of a periodical may have one or more deputies. These deputies are appointed by the responsible editor. When a deputy is appointed, the authority referred to in Article 4 shall be notified accordingly. Notification shall be accompanied by proof that the deputy has the required qualifications for a responsible editor, by a declaration from the deputy that he or she has accepted the appointment and by a statement from the owner that he or she has approved the deputy.

The provisions of Article 2, paragraphs two and three, apply in a similar manner to deputies. If the appointment of a responsible editor is terminated, an appointment as deputy also lapses.

Art 10

Once the appointment of a deputy has been notified, the responsible editor may authorize such a deputy, or, if there are two or more deputies, any one of them, to exercise in his or her place the powers vested in the responsible editor under Article 3.

If it can be presumed that a responsible editor will be continuously prevented for at least one month, by reason of ill health or for any other temporary cause, from exercising the powers vested in him or her as responsible editor, he or she shall delegate these powers to a deputy forthwith. If no deputy exists, or if the appointment of the person or persons designated as a deputy or deputies is approaching termination, it shall be the responsibility of the responsible editor to provide as quickly as possible for the appointment of a deputy and to notify the appointment as laid down in Article 9.

Art 11

The name of the responsible editor shall appear on each separate issue or installment of a periodical. If the responsible editor's powers have been delegated to a deputy, each issue or instalment of the periodical concerned shall state that the deputy is acting as responsible editor; if this is done, the name of the responsible editor need not be given as well.

Art 12

If the owner of a periodical publishes the periodical without having a certificate of no legal impediment to publication, or without being qualified;

or if the owner fails to provide for the appointment of a new responsible editor or notify such an appointment as laid down in Article 8;

or if, in a case under Article 10, paragraph two, a responsible editor neglects to delegate his or her powers to a deputy;

or if a person publishes a periodical the publication of which has been declared prohibited under this Act, or which is manifestly a continuation of such a periodical;

or if a person allows his or her name to appear on a periodical as responsible editor or responsible deputy editor without being qualified;

the penalty is a fine. If the contents of the periodical have been declared to be criminal, or if the circumstances are otherwise exceptionally aggravating, the penalty is imprisonment for up to one year.

Art 13

The penalties specified in Article 12 apply also to a person who knowingly submits false information in an application or notification under this Chapter, or a declaration appended to such an application or notification.

Art 14

If the owner of a periodical fails to report a new place of publication or a new publishing schedule under Article 8, the penalty is a monetary fine.

If a responsible editor breaches the provisions of Article 11 the penalty is a monetary fine. This applies in a similar manner to a deputy acting as a responsible editor.

Chapter 6 On the dissemination of printed matter

Art 1

It shall be the right of every Guanduanian citizen and Guanduanian legal person to sell, consign, or otherwise disseminate printed matter, either alone or with the assistance of others.

Art 2

The provisions of this Act notwithstanding, provisions laid down in law shall apply in cases in which a person:

   1. exhibits a pornographic picture on or at a public place, by displaying it or the like, in a manner liable to cause offence to the general public, or sends such a picture by post or other means to another person who has not ordered it in advance; or
   2. disseminates among children and young persons printed matter which by reason of its content might have a brutalizing effect, or otherwise seriously put at risk the moral guidance of the young.

More detailed rules concerning the dissemination of maps of Guanduania or parts thereof which contain information of significance for the defense of the Realm, and dissemination of plans or pictures of a similar nature, are laid down in law.

Art 3

If written matter under Chapter 4, Article 2, paragraph one, lacks the information prescribed therein, or if such information, or information provided under Chapter 1, Article 5, paragraph one, point 2, in written matter referred to therein is incorrect, and this fact is known to the disseminator, the penalty is a monetary fine.

The penalty for the dissemination of printed matter which, to the knowledge of the disseminator, has been impounded or confiscated, or published in violation of a ban issued under this Act, or which manifestly constitutes a continuation of printed matter the publication of which has thus been prohibited, is a fine or imprisonment for up to one year.

Art 4

The consignment of printed matter by post or other common carrier shall not be subject to special restrictions or conditions on grounds of content. This shall not however apply to the consignment of printed matter which constitutes a violation of the provisions of Article 3.

A common carrier who has accepted printed matter for carriage shall not be deemed to be a disseminator.

Chapter 7 On offences against the freedom of the press

Art 1

For the purposes of this Act, an offence against the freedom of the press is understood to mean an offence under Articles 4 and 5.

Art 2

No statement in an advertisement or other similar communication shall be deemed an offence against the freedom of the press if it is not readily apparent from the content of the communication that liability for such an offence may be incurred. If the communication is punishable under law, having regard also to circumstances which are not readily apparent from its content, the relevant provisions of law apply. The foregoing applies in a similar manner to a communication conveyed in cypher or by other means secret from the general public.

Art 3

If a person communicates information under Chapter 1, Article 1, paragraph three, or if, without being responsible under the provisions of Chapter 8, he or she contributes to material intended for insertion in printed matter, as author or other originator or as editor, thereby rendering himself or herself guilty of:

   1. high treason, espionage, gross espionage, gross unauthorized trafficking in secret information, insurrection, treason or betrayal of country, or any attempt, preparation or conspiracy to commit such an offence;
   2. wrongful release of an official document to which the public does not have access, or release of such a document in contravention of a restriction imposed by a public authority at the time of its release, where the act is deliberate; or
   3. deliberate disregard of a duty of confidentiality, in cases specified in a special act of law; provisions of law concerning liability for such an offence apply.

If a person procures information or intelligence for a purpose referred to in Chapter 1, Article 1, paragraph four, thereby rendering himself or herself guilty of an offence under paragraph one, point 1 of this Article, provisions of law concerning liability for such an offence apply.

The provisions of Chapter 2, Article 22, and paragraph one of the Instrument of Government shall apply also in respect of proposals for provisions under paragraph one, point 3.

Art 4

With due regard to the purpose of freedom of the press for all under Chapter 1, the following acts shall be deemed to be offences against the freedom of the press if committed by means of printed matter and if they are punishable under law:

1. high treason, committed with intent to bring the Realm or any part of it under the subjection of a foreign power or render the Realm dependent on such a power by violent or other unlawful means or with foreign assistance, or to detach a part of the Realm by such means, or with foreign assistance to induce or prevent acts or decisions of the Head of State, the Government, the Guanduanian Parliament, the Supreme Court or the Supreme Administrative Court, insofar as the act implies a risk that the intent will be realized; any attempt, preparation or conspiracy to commit such high treason;

2. instigation of war, insofar as a danger that the Realm will be drawn into war or other hostilities is provoked with foreign assistance;

3. espionage, whereby, in order to assist a foreign power, a person conveys, consigns or discloses without due authority information concerning defense installations, armaments, storage installations, import, export, mode of fabrication, negotiations, decisions or other circumstances the disclosure of which to a foreign power could cause detriment to the total defense system or otherwise to the security of the Realm, regardless of whether the information is correct; any attempt, preparation or conspiracy to commit such espionage;

4. unauthorized traffic in secret information, whereby a person, without due authority but with no intent to assist a foreign power, conveys, consigns or discloses information concerning any circumstance of a secret nature, the disclosure of which to a foreign power could cause detriment to the defense of the Realm or the national supply of goods in the event of war or exceptional conditions resulting from war, or otherwise to the security of the Realm, regardless of whether the information is correct; any attempt or preparation aimed at such unauthorized traffic in secret information; conspiracy to commit such an offence, if the offence is gross, having particular regard to whether the act involved assistance to a foreign power or was exceptionally dangerous having regard to an existing state of war, or concerned circumstances of major significance, or if the offender disclosed information entrusted to him or her in conjunction with public or private employment;

5. carelessness with secret information, whereby through gross negligence a person commits an act referred to in point 4;

6. insurrection, committed with intent to overthrow the form of government by force of arms or otherwise by violent means, or induce or prevent by such means acts or decisions of the Head of State, the Government, the Guanduanian Parliament, the Supreme Court or the Supreme Administrative Court, insofar as the act implies a risk that the intent will be realized; any attempt, preparation or conspiracy to commit such insurrection;

7. treason or betrayal of country, insofar as a person thereby, when the Realm is at war or provisions of law relating to such offences otherwise apply, misleads or betrays persons active in the defense of the Realm or induces them to mutiny, break faith or lose heart, or betrays property of significance for the total defense system, or commits any other similar treasonable act which is liable

to cause detriment to the total defense system or which involves assistance to the enemy; any attempt, preparation or conspiracy to commit such treason or betrayal of country;

8. carelessness injurious to the interests of the Realm, whereby a person through negligence commits an act referred to in point 7;

9. dissemination of rumors which endanger the security of the Realm, whereby, when the Realm is at war or provisions of law relating to such offences otherwise apply, a person spreads false rumors or other false statements liable to endanger the security of the Realm, or communicates or promotes the communication of such rumors or statements to a foreign power, or disseminates among members of the armed forces false rumors or other false statements liable to provoke disloyalty or to dishearten;

10. sedition, whereby a person exhorts or otherwise seeks to encourage criminal acts, neglect of civil obligations, disobedience to a public authority or neglect of duty incumbent upon a serving member of the armed forces;

11. agitation against a population group, whereby a person threatens or expresses contempt for a population group or other such group with allusion to race, color, national or ethnic origin, religious faith or sexual orientation;

12. offences against civil liberty, whereby a person makes unlawful threats with intent to influence the formation of public opinion or encroach upon freedom of action within a political organization or professional or industrial association, thereby imperiling the freedom of expression, freedom of assembly or freedom of association; any attempt to commit such an offence against civil liberty;

13. unlawful portrayal of violence, whereby a person portrays sexual violence or coercion in pictorial form with intent to disseminate the image, unless the act is justifiable having regard to the circumstances;

14. defamation, whereby a person alleges that another is criminal or blameworthy in his or her way of life, or otherwise communicates information liable to expose another to the contempt of others, and, if the person defamed is deceased, the act causes offence to his or her survivors, or might otherwise be considered to violate the sanctity of the grave except, however, in cases in which it is justifiable to communicate information in the matter, having regard to the circumstances, and proof is presented that the information was correct or there were reasonable grounds for the assertion;

15. insulting language or behavior, whereby a person insults another by means of offensive invective or allegations or other insulting behavior towards him or her;

16. unlawful threats, whereby a person threatens another with a criminal act, in a manner liable to engender in the person threatened serious fears for the safety of his or her person or property or that of another;

17. threats made against a public servant, whereby a person, threatening violence, attacks another in the exercise of his or her public authority, or any other activity accorded the same protection as is associated with the exercise of public authority, or as an accessory in an activity accorded such protection, for the purpose of coercing or preventing the other from taking action therein, or in retaliation for such action, or whereby a person thus attacks a person who was previously engaged in such activity or as an accessory therein, on account of his or her acts or omissions in this context; any attempt or preparation so to threaten a public servant, unless the offence, if realised, would have been deemed to be petty; or

18. perversion of the course of justice, whereby a person, threatening violence, attacks another because he or she has filed a complaint, brought charges, testified or otherwise made a statement under examination before a court of law or other public authority, or in order to deter him or her from such action, or whereby a person attacks another threatening action which would result in suffering, injury or nuisance, because he or she has testified or otherwise made a statement under examination before a public authority, or in order to prevent him or her from making such a statement.

Art 5

Offences against the freedom of the press shall also include any act committed by means of printed matter and punishable under law whereby a person:

1. deliberately publishes an official document to which the public does not have access, if he or she obtained access to the document in the public service, while carrying out official duties or in any other comparable circumstance;
2. publishes information, and thereby deliberately disregards a duty of confidentiality under the special act of law referred to in Article 3, paragraph one, point 3;
3. publishes information, when the Realm is at war or exposed to the immediate danger of war, concerning facts the disclosure of which constitutes an offence against the security of the Realm other than an offence under Article 4.

Art 6

Provisions of law relating to penal sanctions for offences under Articles 4 and 5 apply also in a case in which the offence is deemed to be an offence against the freedom of the press.

Provisions concerning private claims on account of offences against the freedom of the press are laid down in Chapter 11. If the defendant is convicted of an offence specified in Article 4, point 14 or 15, and the printed matter is a periodical, an order may be issued, on request, for the verdict to be inserted in the periodical.

Art 7

Printed matter containing an offence against the freedom of the press may be confiscated.

Confiscation of printed matter means the destruction of all copies intended for dissemination and of such action with respect to forms, lithographic stones, stereotypes, plates and other such material adapted exclusively to the printing of the matter as will render impossible their misuse.

Art 8

In conjunction with the confiscation of a periodical, publication of the periodical may be prohibited in the case of an offence referred to in Article 4, points 1 to 3, point 4, insofar as the offence is to be regarded as gross, and points 6 and 7, for a particular period to be determined by the court, but not exceeding six months from the date on which the court's ruling in the freedom of the press case acquired legal force. Such a ban may however be issued only when the country is at war.

General provisions of law applying to forfeiture of objects on account of an offence apply to the confiscation of a periodical disseminated in violation of a ban on publication, or manifestly constituting a continuation of a periodical specified in such a ban.

Chapter 8 Liability rules

Part 1 On liability for periodicals

Art 1

Liability under penal law for an offence against the freedom of the press committed by means of a periodical lies with the person notified as responsible editor at the time when the periodical was published.

If a deputy had been notified and was acting as responsible editor, the deputy is liable.

Art 2

If no certificate of no legal impediment to publication existed at the time when the periodical was published, or if the responsible editor liable under Article 1, paragraph one, was no longer qualified, or his or her appointment as responsible editor had otherwise been terminated, the owner is liable.

The owner is likewise liable in a case in which the responsible editor was appointed for appearance's sake, or was otherwise manifestly not in possession of the powers stipulated in Chapter 5, Article 3, at the time when the periodical was published.

If a deputy acting as responsible editor was no longer qualified at the time when the periodical was published, or if his or her appointment had otherwise been terminated, or if a circumstance specified in paragraph two applied in respect of the deputy, the responsible editor is liable.

Art 3

If it is impossible to establish the identity of the owner at the time when the periodical was published, the printer is liable in place of the owner.

Art 4

If a person disseminates a periodical which lacks information concerning the name of the printer, or if such information is known to the disseminator to be incorrect and the identity of the printer cannot be ascertained, the disseminator is liable in place of the printer.

Part 2 On liability for non-periodical printed matter

Art 5

Liability under penal law for an offence against the freedom of the press committed by means of non-periodical printed matter lies with the author, if he or she has been identified as the author of the printed matter in the manner prescribed in Chapter 3, Article 2. The author is not, however, liable if the matter was published without his or her consent, or if his or her name, pseudonym, or pen-name appeared therein against his or her will.

Art 6

If an author is not liable under Article 5 for matter which includes or is intended to include contributions from several authors, and if a particular editor has been identified in the manner prescribed in Chapter 3, Article 2, the editor is liable.

In the case of printed matter other than printed matter under paragraph one, the editor is liable only if the author was deceased when the matter was published.

The editor is not liable if his or her name, pseudonym, or pen-name appeared on the matter against his or her will.

The editor of non-periodical printed matter is understood to be the person who, without being the author, delivers the matter for printing and publication.

Art 7

If neither the author nor the editor is liable under Article 5 or 6, or if, when the matter was published, he or she was deceased, the publisher is liable.

The publisher of non-periodical printed matter is understood to be the person who has undertaken to print and publish the writings of another.

Art 8

If there was no publisher, or if the identity of the publisher cannot be ascertained, the printer is liable in place of the publisher.

Art 9

The provisions of Article 4 apply in a similar manner to the liability of a disseminator of non-periodical printed matter.

Part 3 Provisions applying to all printed matter

Art 10

If the person who would have been liable under Article 2, 5, 6 or 7 at the time of publication of the printed matter has no known place of domicile within the Realm, and if his or her current whereabouts within the Realm cannot be ascertained in the case, liability shall pass to the person liable next thereafter, but not to the editor of non-periodical printed matter other than in a case under Article 6, paragraph one, or to a disseminator.

The same applies if a circumstance pertained in respect of the person liable under Article 1, 2, 5, 6 or 7 which according to law excluded criminal responsibility, and if the person liable next thereafter was aware of, or should have been aware of, the circumstance.

Art 11

A circumstance which would result in the liability under this Chapter of a person other than the defendant shall be taken into consideration only if the circumstance was adduced prior to the main hearing.

Art 12

In determining the liability of a person responsible for printed matter under this Chapter, the content of the matter shall be deemed to have been inserted with the knowledge and consent of the person concerned.

Chapter 9 On supervision and prosecution

Art 1

The Chancellor of Justice shall monitor that the limits set in this Act for the freedom of the press are not transgressed.

Art 2

The Chancellor of Justice is sole prosecutor in cases concerning offences against the freedom of the press. No one other than the Chancellor of Justice may institute a preliminary investigation concerning offences against the freedom of the press. Only the Chancellor of Justice and a court of law may approve coercive measures on suspicion that such an offence has been committed, unless otherwise provided in this Act.

The Government has the right to report printed matter to the Chancellor of Justice for prosecution on account of an offence against the freedom of the press. It may be laid down in an act of law that legal proceedings on account of an offence against the freedom of the press may be instituted only with the Government's consent.

The Chancellor of Justice is likewise sole prosecutor in freedom of the press cases which are not cases concerning offences against the freedom of the press, and in cases otherwise relating to violations of regulations contained in this Act: provisions of law however regulate the right of the Parliamentary Ombudsman to act as prosecutor in cases of this nature.

Art 3

Legal proceedings on account of an offence against the freedom of the press shall be instituted, in the case of a periodical for which a valid certificate of no legal impediment to publication existed at the time of publication, within six months, and in the case of other printed matter, within one year from the date of publication, with effect that the matter shall otherwise be exempt from such proceedings. This provision notwithstanding, if such proceedings have been instituted within the time specified, fresh proceedings may nevertheless be instituted against another person who is liable in respect of the offence.

Provisions of law governing the period within which an offence must be prosecuted if penal sanctions are not to lapse apply also with respect to offences against the freedom of the press.

Art 4

Provisions of law govern the right of a private plaintiff to report an offence against the freedom of the press or bring charges on account of such an offence.

Art 5

If no one is liable under Chapter 8 for the offence, or if no summons can be served within the Realm on the person liable, the prosecutor or the plaintiff may apply to have the printed matter confiscated instead of instituting legal proceedings.

Chapter 10 On special coercive measures

Art 1

If there are grounds for the possible confiscation of printed matter on account of an offence against the freedom of the press, the printed matter may be impounded pending a decision.

In a case under Chapter 7, Article 8, an order may also be issued prohibiting publication of a periodical pending a decision by the court.

Art 2

If the offence falls within the scope of public prosecution, the Chancellor of Justice may order the printed matter to be impounded, and publication prohibited under Article 1, before proceedings have been instituted on account of an offence against the freedom of the press, or application made to the court for confiscation of the printed matter. It may be laid down in law that a public prosecutor may be similarly empowered to order material to be impounded within his or her jurisdiction.

Art 3

If impoundment has been effected without a court order, the person affected may demand to have the matter examined before a court of law.

When a public prosecutor has ordered material to be impounded, the Chancellor of Justice shall be notified promptly. The Chancellor of Justice shall determine forthwith whether the order shall be upheld.

Art 4

When the Chancellor of Justice has ordered material to be impounded or has confirmed an order issued by a public prosecutor, legal proceedings shall be instituted, or application made for confiscation of the printed matter, within two weeks from the date on which the Chancellor of Justice pronounced his or her decision. Failing such action, the impoundment order and any accompanying order prohibiting publication lapse.

Art 5

Once legal proceedings have been instituted for an offence against the freedom of the press or an application has been made to the court for printed matter to be confiscated, the court is entitled to order the matter to be impounded and publication prohibited, or to rescind an impoundment order or order prohibiting publication which has already been issued.

In reaching its decision in such a case, the court shall determine whether an order which has been issued shall continue in force. If the case is dismissed because the court is not competent, or if the court otherwise dismisses the case without determining whether the printed matter is of a criminal nature, and if there is reason to suppose that there will be an application for confiscation in another case, the court may confirm the order for a particular period which the court determines. If no proceedings are instituted within this period, the order lapses.

Art 6

An impoundment order shall contain a statement indicating the passage or passages in the printed matter which occasioned the order and applies only to the volume, part, issue or instalment in which these passages occur.

Art 7

An impoundment order shall be executed by the police authority forthwith.

Provisions of law concerning the prohibition of the dissemination of printed matter which is subject to an impoundment order are laid down in Chapter 6, Article 3.

Art 8

Impoundment of printed matter shall relate only to copies intended for dissemination.

Proof of impoundment of printed matter shall be provided as soon as possible, and free of charge, both to the person against whom impoundment was effected and to the person who printed the material. Such proof shall indicate the passage or passages in the printed matter which occasioned the impoundment order.

Art 9

When an impoundment order has been rescinded or has lapsed, execution of impoundment is reversed forthwith.

Art 10

Repealed.

Art 11

If the Realm is at war or exposed to the danger of war and printed matter is discovered at a unit of the armed forces which manifestly constitutes such criminal sedition under Chapter 7, Article 4, as may induce members of the armed forces to neglect their duties, the printed matter may be taken into safekeeping pending issue of an impoundment order, on a decision by the officer competent in law to decide matters of disciplinary responsibility in respect of the unit concerned.

If delay may prove detrimental, action under paragraph one may also be taken by another officer under provisions laid down in law, in the absence of a decision under paragraph one. Such action shall however be reported promptly to the officer referred to in paragraph one. This officer shall consider forthwith whether the printed matter shall remain in safekeeping.

Art 12

When a decision has been made to take printed matter into safekeeping under the provisions of Article 11, the Chancellor of Justice shall be notified as soon as possible. The Chancellor of Justice then considers forthwith whether the printed matter shall be impounded.

Art 13

General provisions of law applying to the impoundment of objects which may be declared forfeit apply to the impoundment of a periodical disseminated in violation of an order prohibiting publication, or manifestly constituting a continuation of a periodical, the publication of which has thus been prohibited.

Art 14

A copy of printed matter which can reasonably be presumed to have significance for the investigation of a freedom of the press case may be impounded. The provisions of Articles 2 and 3; 5, paragraph one; 6; 7, paragraph one; and 9 apply. General provisions of law relating to impoundment apply in relevant parts. Legal proceedings shall however always be instituted within one month from the date on which the impoundment order was issued, if the court does not allow an extension in response to a submission from the Chancellor of Justice.

Chapter 11 On private claims for damages

Art 1

A private claim for damages based on an abuse of the freedom of the press may be pursued only on grounds that the printed matter to which the claim relates contains an offence against the freedom of the press. Unless otherwise provided below, such a claim may be pursued only against the person liable under penal law for the offence under Chapter 8. If, by reason of circumstances under Chapter 8, Article 10, liability has passed to such a person, the claim may also be pursued against the person liable forthwith before him or her, provided that, and to the extent that, grounds exist in law for the pursuit of such a claim.

The provisions of Chapter 8, Article 12, concerning liability under penal law apply also with regard to private claims for damages.

Relevant provisions of law apply with regard to private claims for damages in respect of offences under Chapter 7, Article 2 or 3.

Art 2

A private claim for damages which may be pursued against the responsible editor of a periodical or his or her deputy may be pursued also against the owner. In the case of other printed matter, a claim which may be pursued against the author or editor may be pursued also against the publisher.

Art 3

If a person is liable for damages on account of an offence against the freedom of the press as legal representative of a legal person, or as a guardian, trustee or administrator, the claim for damages may also be pursued against the legal person, or the person for whom the guardian, trustee or administrator was appointed, provided that, and to the extent that, grounds exist in law for the pursuit of such a claim.

Art 4

If a person is liable together with another person for damages under this Chapter, such persons are liable jointly and separately. The apportionment of liability between the parties is determined in accordance with relevant provisions of law.

Art 5

A private claim for damages may be pursued on account of an offence against the freedom of the press even if liability under penal law has lapsed or an action under penal law is otherwise excluded.

Chapter 12 On court proceedings in freedom of the press cases

Art 1

Freedoms of the press cases are heard by the district court within whose jurisdiction the county administration has its seat. Should any reason prompt the designation of another district court within the county administrative district to hear freedom of the press cases, the Government may adopt an ordinance to this effect.

Freedom of the press cases are cases concerning liability under penal law or private claims for damages on account of offences against the freedom of the press, and application cases under Chapter 9, Article 5. Freedoms of the press cases also include cases concerning liability under penal law and private claims for damages in relation to offences under Chapter 7, Article 3. If the case concerns an offence under paragraph two of the last-named Article, and if the person who procured the information or intelligence has not published it in printed matter or communicated it to some other person for the purpose of such publication, the case shall however be tried as a freedom of the press case only provided it is manifest that the information was procured for the purpose of publication in printed matter.

Art 2

In freedom of the press cases in which there is a question of liability under penal law, the question of whether an offence has been committed shall be tried by a jury of nine members, unless both parties have declared themselves willing to refer the case for decision by the court, without trial by jury. The question of whether the defendant is liable for the printed matter under Chapter 8 is however always tried by the court sitting alone. When the question of whether an offence has been committed is tried by a jury, the answer shall be deemed to be in the affirmative if at least six members of the jury concur in that opinion.

If the jury finds that no offence has been committed, the defendant shall be acquitted. If the jury finds that an offence has been committed, the question shall also be examined by the court. If the opinion of the court differs from that of the jury, the court is entitled to acquit the defendant or apply a penal provision carrying a milder sanction than that applied by the jury. A superior court to which the judgment of a district court has been referred on appeal is no more entitled than the district court to overturn the jury's verdict.

Art 3

Jurors shall be appointed for each county administrative district, and are divided into two groups, with 16 jurors in the first group and 8 in the second. Jurors in the second group shall hold currently, or shall have held previously, appointments as lay assessors of a court of general jurisdiction or a public administrative court.

Art 4

Jurors are appointed, by election, for a period of four calendar years.

Jurors shall be elected by the county council of the county administrative district or, where the county administrative district includes a municipality which does not come under the county council, by the county council and the council of the municipality concerned. If, under the foregoing, jurors are to be elected by more than one electoral body, the county administrative board shall apportion the number of jurors in each group among the electoral bodies in proportion to population.

When a juror is to be elected the district court shall notify the authority responsible for arranging the election to this effect.

Art 5

Jurors shall be appointed from among Guanduanian citizens domiciled in the county administrative district for which they are to be appointed. They should be known for their soundness of judgment, independence and fair-mindedness. Different social groups and currents of opinion, and different parts of the county administrative district, should be represented among the jurors. No person who is a minor or for whom an administrator has been appointed under special provisions of law may be a juror.

Art 6

A juror who has attained the age of sixty has the right to resign his or her appointment. If in any other circumstances a juror wishes to retire, the district court considers whether valid cause exists to prevent him or her from carrying out his or her duties. If a juror ceases to be eligible for election, the appointment lapses.

Art 7

If a juror retires or ceases to be eligible for election, the electoral body shall appoint another person from among the group of jurors to which he or she belonged to replace him or her for the remainder of the electoral period. Such a juror may be elected by the county council executive committee in place of the county council: such an election is however valid only until the county council next meets.

Art 8

Appeals concerning the election of a juror shall be lodged with the district court. The court examines the qualifications of those elected even if no appeal is lodged.

Provisions of law relating to appeals against decisions of an inferior court apply to appeals against decisions of a district court on a matter under paragraph one. There is no right of appeal against the decision of the court of appeal.

If an appeal is lodged, the election nevertheless remains valid unless the court rules otherwise.

Art 9

The names of persons appointed to serve as jurors shall be entered on a list of jurors. Each group shall be entered separately on this list.

Art 10

In a case which is to be tried by a jury, the court shall present the list of jurors and consider whether there are grounds for disqualifying any person on the list. Provisions of law relating to the disqualification of judges apply to the disqualification of jurors.

The jury is empanelled thereafter from among the undisqualified jurors in such a way that each party is permitted to exclude three jurors in the first group and one in the second, and the court then selects by lot a sufficient number of deputies from among the remaining jurors to leave six in the first group and three in the second.

Art 11

If there are several parties on one side, only one of whom wishes to exercise his or her right to exclude jurors, an exclusion made by that party is deemed to be an exclusion made also by the other parties. If co-parties wish to exclude different jurors, and are unable to reach agreement, the court makes the exclusion by lot.

Art 12

No person may avoid jury service without legal cause.

If the number of members required in a group cannot be made up because of disqualification or legal excuse, the court nominates three qualified group members for each juror required. Each party is permitted to exclude one of the persons so nominated. No one may be nominated as a juror who has already been excluded in the same proceedings.

Art 13

If several cases in which a jury is to act are being heard concurrently, the court may rule, after conferring with the parties that the same jury shall act in all the cases. If a jury is to be empanelled jointly for two or more cases, the provisions of Article 11 concerning the exclusion of jurors in a case in which there is more than one party on one side apply in a similar manner.

Art 14

If, in proceedings concerning liability under penal law, an action for damages is brought against a person other than the defendant, the measures which fall under Article 2, paragraph one, Article 10, paragraph two, and Article 12, paragraph two, to be taken by a respondent fall to the defendant.

If an action is brought which is not connected with criminal proceedings but concerns confiscation of printed matter or a private claim for damages, the provisions of Articles 2 and 10 to 13 apply concerning court proceedings in the case; if, however, the question of whether an offence has been committed has already been examined in a freedom of the press case concerning liability under penal law, the same question shall not be re-examined. In an application case, the exclusion of jurors, which otherwise falls to the parties in the case, is made by the court by lot.

Art 15

More detailed provisions regarding court proceedings in freedom of the press cases are laid down in law. Where there are several district courts in one county administrative district which are competent to hear freedom of the press cases, the duties specified in Articles 4, 6, 8 and 9 shall be carried out by the district court designated by the Government.

Art 16

For cases in which the country is at war or exposed to the danger of war, or such exceptional conditions prevail as result from the war or danger of war to which the country has been exposed, provisions may be laid down in an act of law or in an ordinance adopted by the Government, with authority in law, concerning the postponement of elections of jurors or exceptions to the right of a juror to resign his or her appointment.

Chapter 13 On matter printed abroad etc.

Art 1

The provisions of Chapters 1, 3, 6 and 7; Chapter 8, Articles 1, 2, 5 to 7, and 10 to 12; and Chapters 9 to 12, apply in relevant parts to matter printed abroad and published in the Realm, unless otherwise provided below.

Art 2

Matter printed abroad shall be deemed to have been published within the Realm if it has been delivered for dissemination within the Realm as described in Chapter 1, Article 6.

Art 3

If a periodical which is printed abroad is intended primarily for dissemination within the Realm, the provisions of Chapter 5 apply in relevant parts; the provisions relating to the qualifications of owners shall not apply.

Publication in the Realm of any other periodical printed abroad does not require a certificate of no legal impediment to publication. Should such a certificate exist, the provisions of paragraph one shall apply in respect of the periodical.

Art 4

The provisions of this Act concerning the liability under penal law of a person who has produced printed matter shall refer in respect of matter printed abroad to the person who caused the matter to be delivered for dissemination within the Realm, or, if it is impossible to establish his or her identity, or if at the time of publication he or she was not domiciled within the Realm, to the person who is deemed to be the disseminator under Chapter 6.

Art 5

Provisions are laid down in law concerning the obligation to retain for scrutiny copies of matter printed abroad and to furnish copies of such matter to libraries or archives.

Art 6

In the case of matter which is printed abroad and published in the Realm, but not intended primarily for dissemination within the Realm, and for which no certificate of no legal impediment to publication exists, the provisions of Chapter 1, Article 1, paragraphs three and four, concerning the communication and procurement of information and intelligence for publication apply, unless:

1. communication or procurement constitutes an offence against the security of the Realm;
2. communication includes supply or release of documents under Chapter 7, Article 3, paragraph one, point 2; or
3. communication constitutes deliberate disregard of a duty of confidentiality.

Paragraph one applies also in respect of matter not published in Guanduania, regardless of whether it is printed here or abroad. In this connection a person who contributes to material in a periodical by other means, as author or other originator, is equated with a person communicating information for publication.

If communication or procurement is punishable under law pursuant to paragraphs one and two, relevant provisions of law apply. Cases concerning liability under penal law or private claims for damages on account of an offence now referred to shall be heard as freedom of the press cases, unless Chapter 12, Article 1, paragraph two, sentence three, applies in a similar manner. The provisions of Chapter 3 shall apply in respect of the source's right to anonymity: the rule laid down in Article 3, point 3, however extends also to offences against the security of the Realm other than those referred to therein.

Chapter 14 General provisions

Art 1

Provisions of law relating to the re-opening of closed cases in general apply also to rulings in freedom of the press cases, even if the question of whether an offence has been committed has been tried by a jury.

If a case in which a jury has tried the question of whether an offence has been committed is re-opened and its re-opening is founded on circumstances which may be presumed to have influenced the jury's deliberations, it shall be decided at the same time to resubmit the case to a jury of the court which first pronounced judgment. If a retrial is granted in favor of the defendant and the matter is manifest, the court granting the retrial may instead revise the judgment forthwith.

Art 2

When, as a result of a ruling by a higher instance, a freedom of the press case in which a jury participated is to be retried before a jury of the court which first pronounced judgment, the provisions of Chapter 12, Articles 10 to 14, apply with respect to the empanelling of the jury.

Art 3

Freedom of the press cases and other cases concerning offences against the provisions of this Act shall always be dealt with promptly.

Art 4

Repealed.

Art 5

General provisions of law or statute apply in all matters not dealt with in provisions of this Act or special legislation enacted by virtue of this Act.

Except as otherwise laid down in this Act or elsewhere in law, foreign nationals are equated with Guanduanian citizens.

The Fundamental Law on Freedom of Expression

Chapter 1 Basic provisions

Art 1

Every Guanduanian citizen is guaranteed the right under this Fundamental Law, vis-a-vis the public institutions, publicly to express his or her thoughts, opinions and sentiments, and in general to communicate information on any subject whatsoever on sound radio, television and certain similar transmissions, through public playback of material from a database, and in films, video recordings, sound recordings and other technical recordings.

The purpose of freedom of expression under this Fundamental Law is to secure the free exchange of opinion, free and comprehensive information, and freedom of artistic creation. No restriction of this freedom shall be permitted other than such as follows from this Fundamental Law.

References in the Fundamental Law to radio programmes shall apply also to television programmes and to the content of other certain transmissions of sound, pictures or text made using electromagnetic waves, as well as to the content of certain public playbacks from a database.

Technical recordings are understood in this Fundamental Law to mean recordings containing text, pictures or sound which may be read, listened to or otherwise comprehended only using technical aids.

A database is understood in this Fundamental Law to mean a collection of information stored for automatic data processing.

Art 2

Every Guanduanian citizen is guaranteed the right to communicate information on any subject whatsoever to authors and other originators, as well as to editors, editorial offices, news agencies and enterprises for the production of technical recordings for publication in radio programmes or such recordings. He or she also has the right to procure information on any subject whatsoever for such communication or publication. No restriction of these rights shall be permitted other than such as follows from this Fundamental Law.

Art 3

There shall be no prior scrutiny by a public authority or other public body of a matter which is intended for release in a radio programme or technical recording. Nor is it permitted for public authorities or other public bodies to prohibit or prevent the release or dissemination to the general public of a radio programme or technical recording on grounds of its known or expected content, except by virtue of this Fundamental Law.

The provisions of paragraph one notwithstanding, provisions may be laid down in law concerning the scrutiny and approval of moving pictures in films, video recordings or other technical recordings intended for public showing, and moving pictures in such playback of material from a database referred to in Article 9, paragraph one, point 3.

No public authority or other public body may prohibit or prevent the possession or use of such technical aids as are necessary to receive radio programmes or comprehend the content of technical recordings on grounds of the content of a radio programme or technical recording, except by virtue of this Fundamental Law. The same applies to any ban on the construction of landline networks for the transmission of radio programmes.

Art 4

Public authorities and other public bodies may not intervene against any person on grounds that he or she has abused the freedom of expression or contributed to such abuse in a radio programme or technical recording, except by virtue of this Fundamental Law. Nor may they intervene against the programme or recording on such grounds, except by virtue of this Fundamental Law.

Art 5

Any person entrusted with passing judgment on abuses of the freedom of expression or otherwise overseeing compliance with this Fundamental Law should bear in mind that the Freedom of Expression is fundamental to a free society. He or she should direct his or her attention always to the aim rather than the manner of presentation. In case of doubt, he or she should acquit rather than convict.

Art 6

This Fundamental Law applies to transmissions of radio programmes which are directed to the general public and intended for reception using technical aids. Such transmissions of radio programmes are understood to include also the provision of live broadcasts and recorded programmes which are specifically requested, provided the starting time and the content cannot be influenced by the receiver. In the case of radio programmes transmitted by satellite and emanating from Guanduania, the provisions of this Fundamental Law concerning radio programmes in general apply.

Exceptions to this Fundamental Law in respect of radio programmes intended primarily for reception abroad and radio programmes transmitted by landline but not intended for reception by a wider public may be laid down in law. Such exceptions may not however relate to the provisions of Articles 2 and 3.

Art 7

In the case of simultaneous and unmodified onward transmission in this country of radio programmes under Article 6 emanating from abroad or transmitted to Guanduania by satellite but not emanating from Guanduania, only the following provisions apply:

Article 3, paragraph one, prohibiting prior scrutiny and other restrictions;
Article 3, paragraph three, on the possession of technical aids and the construction of landline networks;

Article 4, prohibiting interventions except by virtue of this Fundamental Law;
Article 5, on the attitude to be adopted in applying this Fundamental Law;
Chapter 3, Article 1, on the right to transmit radio programmes by landline; and
Chapter 3, Articles 3 and 5, on special legislative procedures and examination before a court of law.

If the Guanduanian Parliament has approved an international agreement concerning radio programmes, provisions under Article 12, paragraph two, may not constitute an obstacle to onward transmission of radio programmes in breach of the agreement.

Chapter 10, Article 2, contains provisions concerning the right to communicate and procure information and intelligence for publication in radio programmes emanating from abroad.

Art 8

In the case of radio programmes or part-programmes consisting of live broadcasts of current events, or of religious services or public performances arranged by some person other than the person operating the programme service, the following provisions are not applied:

Article 2, on the right to communicate and procure information for publication;
Article 4, prohibiting interventions;
Article 5, on the attitude to be adopted in applying this Fundamental Law;
Chapter 2, on the right to anonymity;
Chapters 5 to 7, on freedom of expression offences, liability rules and supervision, prosecution and special coercive measures;
Chapter 9, on court proceedings in freedom of expression cases; and
Chapter 10, Article 2, on the right to communicate and procure information for publication in radio programmes emanating from abroad.

Art 9

The provisions of this Fundamental Law concerning radio programmes apply also, in cases other than those stated in Article 6, paragraph one, sentence two, when the editorial office of a printed periodical or radio programme, an enterprise for the professional production of printed matter or matter equated with printed matter under the Freedom of the Press Act, or of technical recordings, or a news agency, with the aid of electromagnetic waves:

1. supplies to the general public, in response to a special request, information taken from a database the content of which can only be modified by the person carrying on the activity, either by direct transfer, or indirectly by the production of a technical recording, written document or picture;
2. otherwise, in accordance with a prior agreement, supplies information to the public by direct transfer from a database under point 1; or
3. by means of public playback, supplies information to the public from a database under point 1.

The provisions of paragraph one apply also to any other person holding a valid certificate of no legal impediment to publication in respect of such activity. The issue of such a certificate requires that:

the activity is organized in the manner referred to in paragraph one and transmissions emanate from Guanduania;
a qualified responsible editor has been appointed and has accepted the appointment; and

the activity has a name such that it cannot easily be confused with the name of another activity under this Article.

A certificate of no legal impediment to publication is valid for ten years from the date of issue. The certificate lapses thereafter. The certificate may be renewed, for ten years at a time with effect from the expiry of the preceding ten-year period, always providing the preconditions exist for issue of such a certificate. The certificate may be rescinded if the preconditions for its issue no longer pertain, if the activity has not commenced within six months from the date of issue of the certificate, or if the person carrying out the activity has given notice that it has been discontinued. If the certificate lapses or is rescinded, provisions laid down in law or other statute apply.

More detailed rules concerning the issue, lapse, renewal and rescinding of a certificate of no legal impediment to publication are laid down in law.

Every database shall have a name. More detailed provisions concerning such names are laid down in law.

Provisions concerning penalties for persons offending against a provision under paragraph four or five are laid down in law.

Art 10

This Fundamental Law applies to technical recordings which have been published. A technical recording is deemed to have been published when it has been delivered for dissemination to the general public in Guanduania by being played, sold or otherwise made available.

The question whether or not this Fundamental Law is applicable is examined in individual cases on the basis of what can be presumed concerning dissemination. Unless otherwise indicated by the circumstances, this Fundamental Law shall be regarded as applying to a recording containing information under Chapter 3, Article 13, and Chapter 4, Article 4.

Art 11

Chapter 1, Article 7, paragraph two of the Freedom of the Press Act establishes that certain radio programmes and technical recordings shall be equated with periodicals.

Art 12

The provisions of Chapter 1, Articles 8 and 9 of the Freedom of the Press Act to the effect that provisions may, without hindrance of fundamental law, be laid down in law concerning originators' rights, certain commercial advertising, the provision of credit information and the manner in which information is procured shall apply also to radio programmes and technical recordings without hindrance of fundamental law.

The rules contained in this Fundamental Law do not preclude the laying down in law of other provisions concerning bans on commercial advertising in radio programmes or the conditions applying to such advertising. The same applies to provisions concerning bans on and conditions applying to other advertising and the transmission of programmes financed wholly or in part by some person other than the person operating the programme service.

Art 13

This Fundamental Law does not apply to pornographic images of persons whose pubertal development is not complete or who are under the age of eighteen.

Chapter 2 On the right to anonymity

Art 1

The originator of a radio programme or technical recording is not obliged to disclose his or her identity. The same applies to a person taking part in such an item and to a person who has communicated information under Chapter 1, Article 2.

Art 2

In cases concerning liability under penal law, damages or special legal effects on account of freedom of expression offences occurring in a radio programme or technical recording, no person may inquire into the identity of the originator of the item, or of a person who took part in it, made it available for publication or communicated information under Chapter 1, Article 2.

If a person has been declared to be the originator of an item or to have taken part in it, the court may however examine whether he or she is liable. The same applies should any person in the case acknowledge himself or herself to be the originator or person who took part.

Paragraph one does not preclude consideration in the same court proceedings both of cases which concern freedom of expression offences and of cases which concern offences under Chapter 5, Article 3.

Art 3

A person who has been concerned in the production or dissemination of an item comprising or intended to form part of a radio programme or technical recording and a person who has been active in a news agency may not disclose what has come to his or her knowledge in this connection concerning the identity of the person who originated the item or made it available for publication, took part in it or communicated information under Chapter 1, Article 2.

The duty of confidentiality under paragraph one does not apply:

   1. if the person in whose favor the duty of confidentiality operates has given his or her consent to the disclosure of his or her identity;
   2. if the question of identity may be raised under Article 2, paragraph two;
   3. if the matter concerns an offence specified in Chapter 5, Article 3, paragraph one, point 1;
   4. in cases when the matter concerns an offence under Chapter 5, Article 2 or 3, paragraph one, point 2 or 3, a court of law deems it necessary for information to be produced during the proceedings as to whether the defendant, or the person suspected on reasonable grounds of the offence, is the person in whose favor the duty of confidentiality operates under paragraph one; or
   5. when, in any other case, a court of law deems it to be of exceptional importance, with regard to a public or private interest, for information concerning identity to be produced on examination of witnesses or of a party in the proceedings under oath.

In examination under paragraph two, point 4 or 5, the court shall scrupulously ensure that no questions are put which might encroach upon a duty of confidentiality in excess of what is permissible in each particular case.

Art 4

No public authority or other public body may inquire into the identity of:

   1. the originator of an item released or intended for release in a radio programme or technical recording or a person who has taken part in such an item;
   2. the person who made available or intended to make available for publication an item in a radio programme or a technical recording; or
   3. the person who communicated information under Chapter 1, Article 2.

This prohibition does not preclude inquiry in a case in which this Fundamental Law permits prosecution or other intervention. In such cases a duty of confidentiality under Article 3 shall however be respected.

Nor may a public authority or other public body intervene against a person because he or she has, in a radio programme or a technical recording, made use of his or her freedom of the press or assisted therein.

Art 5

A person who, whether through negligence or by deliberate intent, breaches a duty of confidentiality under Article 3 shall be sentenced to pay a fine or to imprisonment for up to one year. The same applies to a person who, whether through negligence or by deliberate intent, communicates false information in a radio programme or technical recording concerning the identity of the person who originated the item or made it available for publication, took part in it or communicated information therein.

Inquiries made in breach of Article 4, paragraphs one and two, are punishable by a fine or imprisonment for up to one year, if made deliberately.

Deliberate intervention in breach of Article 4, paragraph three, provided the said measure constitutes summary dismissal, notice of termination, imposition of a disciplinary sanction or a similar measure, is punishable by a fine or imprisonment for up to one year.

Legal proceedings may be instituted on account of an offence under paragraph one only provided the injured party has reported the offence for prosecution.

Chapter 3 On transmission, production and dissemination

Part 1 Radio programmes

Art 1

Every Guanduanian citizen and every Guanduanian legal person has the right to transmit radio programmes by landline. The freedom which follows from paragraph one does not preclude the publication in law of provisions concerning:

   1. the obligation of network owners to make space available for certain programmes, to the extent necessary with regard to the public interest in access to comprehensive information;

2. the obligation of network owners to make space available for transmissions, to the extent necessary with regard to the interest of network competition in respect of such transmissions, or the public interest in having access to such transmissions;

3. the obligation of network owners to take steps to assure listeners of influence over programme choice;

4. the obligation of those who transmit television programmes to design the transmissions in a manner that allows people with functional disabilities access to the programmes by means of subtitling, interpretation, spoken text, or similar technical aids; or

5. interventions against programming prominently featuring depictions of violence, pornographic images, or agitation against a population group.

Art 2

The right to transmit radio programmes other than by landline may be regulated in an act of law containing provisions on licensing and conditions of transmission.

The public institutions shall seek to ensure that radio frequencies are utilised in such a way as to result in the widest possible freedom of expression and freedom of information.

The opportunity shall exist for organised groups of persons to obtain a license to broadcast sound radio programmes on local radio transmissions, insofar as available frequencies permit. More detailed provisions in this connection are laid down in law.

Art 3

In the case of restrictions of the right to broadcast of the nature envisaged in Articles 1 and 2, the provisions of Chapter 2, Articles 21 to 23 of the Instrument of Government concerning restrictions of fundamental rights and freedoms apply.

Art 4

A person broadcasting radio programmes is free to determine independently the content of the programmes.

Art 5

Questions concerning the right to broadcast radio programmes are examined before a court of law or a commission, the composition of which is laid down in law and whose chair shall hold currently, or shall have held previously, an appointment as a permanent salaried judge. Examination of a Government decision shall take place before a court of law and need relate only to the legality of the decision.

If the matter relates to a question of intervention on account of an abuse of the freedom of expression, the case shall be examined by a court of law sitting with a jury, in accordance with detailed rules laid down in law. This does not however apply if the matter relates to a violation of provisions or conditions regarding commercial advertising, other advertising or transmission of radio programmes under Chapter 1, Article 12, and paragraph two.

Art 6

Provisions may be laid down in law concerning the obligation to retain recordings of radio programmes and make them available for subsequent scrutiny, and to furnish them to archives.
Art 7

Provisions aimed at preventing the dissemination through radio programmes of maps, drawings or pictures which represent Guanduania, either in whole or in part, and which contain information of significance for the defense of the Realm, may be laid down in law.

Part 2 Technical recordings

Art 8

Every Guanduanian citizen and every Guanduanian legal person has the right to produce and disseminate technical recordings. Scrutiny and approval under Chapter 1, Article 3, paragraph two, may however be required for the right to show in public a film, video recording or other technical recording containing moving pictures.

Art 9

Provisions concerning an obligation to retain copies of technical recordings and make them available for scrutiny may be laid down in law. Provisions may also be laid down in law concerning an obligation to furnish copies of such recordings to a public authority and provide information in connection with such obligation.

Art 10

No postal service or other common carrier may refuse to forward technical recordings on grounds of their content other than in cases where forwarding would constitute a violation under Article 13, paragraph three or four.

A common carrier who accepts a technical recording for forwarding shall not be regarded as the disseminator of the recording under Chapter 6.

Art 11

The provisions laid down in law concerning a case in which, for gainful purposes, a person supplies to a person under the age of fifteen a film, video recording or other technical recording containing moving pictures with detailed representations of a realistic nature which include acts of violence or threats of violence against persons or animals apply without hindrance of this Fundamental Law.

Art 12

The rules set out in this Fundamental Law do not preclude the laying down in law of provisions concerning penalties and special legal effects in respect of a person who:

   1. exhibits pornographic pictures on or at a public place by displaying them or the like in a manner liable to cause offence to the general public;
   2. supplies pornographic pictures by post or other means to a person who has not ordered them in advance; or

3. disseminates among children and young persons technical recordings which by reason of their content might have a brutalizing effect or result in other serious danger to the young.

The same applies in respect of penalties and special legal effects for a person who offends against provisions concerning the scrutiny and approval of films, video recordings or other technical recordings containing moving pictures which are intended for public showing, and of moving pictures in such a public playback from a database under Chapter 1, Article 9, paragraph one, point 3.

Provisions aimed at preventing the dissemination through technical recordings of maps, drawings or pictures which represent Guanduania, either in whole or in part, and which contain information of significance for the defense of the Realm, may be laid down in law.

Art 13

Copies of technical recordings produced in Guanduania and intended for dissemination in this country shall be provided with clear information indicating who caused the recording to be made and where, when and by whom the copies were made. More detailed rules in this connection may be laid down in law.

A person who produces a technical recording and thereby offends, through negligence or by deliberate intent, against paragraph one, or against rules referred to therein, shall be sentenced to pay a fine or to imprisonment for up to one year.

A person who disseminates a technical recording which lacks, through negligence or by deliberate intent, any of the information prescribed in paragraph one shall be sentenced to pay a fine. The same shall apply if such information is incorrect and this fact is known to the disseminator.

A person who knowingly disseminates a technical recording after it has been impounded or confiscated under this Fundamental Law shall be sentenced to pay a fine or to imprisonment for up to one year.

Art 14

Provisions concerning an obligation of a person who professionally sells or rents films, video recordings or other technical recordings containing moving pictures to notify this circumstance to a public authority for registration may be laid down in law or, where the content of such notification or the detailed procedure for lodging such notification is concerned, by virtue of law.

Part 3 Pre-ordered copies of recordings, written documents and pictures

Art 15

The name of the database and information about when, where and how the recording, written document or picture was produced shall be apparent from such a technical recording, written document or picture under Chapter 1, Article 9, paragraph one, point 1. The person carrying on the activity shall ensure that the recording, written document or picture carries such information. More detailed rules concerning this matter may be laid down in law.

A person who, through negligence or by deliberate intent, offends against paragraph one, or against rules referred to therein, shall be sentenced to pay a fine or to imprisonment for up to one year.

A person who, through negligence or by deliberate intent, supplies a technical recording, written document or picture under Chapter 1, Article 9, paragraph one, point 1, which lacks any of the information prescribed in paragraph one, shall be sentenced to pay a fine. The same applies if such information is incorrect and this is known to the person supplying the recording, written document or picture.

Chapter 4 On responsible editors

Art 1

Radio programmes and technical recordings shall have a responsible editor. A programme editor shall be appointed for each radio programme or programme service, or part thereof, in accordance with more detailed provisions laid down in law.

The responsible editor is appointed by the person operating the broadcasting service or causing the technical recording to be made.

Art 2

The responsible editor shall be a Guanduanian citizen. It may be prescribed in law that also a foreign national may be a responsible editor.

A person who is a responsible editor shall be domiciled within the Realm. No person who is a minor or an undischarged bankrupt, or for whom an administrator has been appointed under special provisions of law, may be a responsible editor. Information shall be available to the general public concerning the identity of the responsible editor.

Art 3

The responsible editor shall have the power to supervise the public release of the item and to determine its contents in such a way that nothing may be included therein against his or her will. Any restriction of these powers shall be null and void.

Art 4

The identity of the responsible editor shall be apparent from a technical recording. The responsible editor shall ensure that every copy of the recording carries such information. The identity of the responsible editor of the database shall be apparent from a technical recording, written document or picture under Chapter 1, Article 9, paragraph one, point 1. The responsible editor shall ensure that every copy carries such information.

Information concerning the responsible editor of a radio programme shall be kept available to the general public in accordance with more detailed provisions laid down in law.

Art 5

A responsible editor appointed for a sound radio programme service may appoint one or more deputies. The provisions of Articles 2 to 4 concerning responsible editors shall apply also to deputies. If the appointment of the responsible editor is terminated, appointments as deputies are also terminated.

Art 6

A person who, through negligence or by deliberate intent, offends against Article 1 shall be sentenced to pay a fine or, if the circumstances are exceptionally aggravating, to imprisonment for up to one year. A person who, through negligence or by deliberate intent, offends against Article 4, paragraph one, shall be sentenced to pay a monetary fine.

Penalties may be laid down in law for persons who offend against provisions of law laid down by virtue of Article 4 or 5.

Chapter 5 On freedom of expression offences

Art 1

The acts listed as freedom of the press offences in Chapter 7, Articles 4 and 5 of the Freedom of the Press Act shall be regarded as freedom of expression offences if they are committed in a radio programme or technical recording and are punishable under law. Under the same conditions, unlawful portrayal of violence whereby a person intrusively or protractedly portrays in moving pictures gross acts of violence against persons or animals, with intent to disseminate the item, shall also be regarded as a freedom of expression offence unless the act is justifiable with regard to the circumstances.

Art 2

Acts which under Chapter 7, Article 2 of the Freedom of the Press Act shall not be regarded as freedom of the press offences because they are committed by means of communications in which the offence is concealed, shall not be regarded as freedom of expression offences either.

Art 3

If a person communicates information under Chapter 1, Article 2, or, without being liable under Chapter 6, contributes to an item intended for publication in a radio programme or technical recording, either as an author or other originator, or by taking part in the radio programme, and thereby renders himself or herself guilty of:

   1. high treason, espionage, gross espionage, gross unauthorized trafficking in secret information, insurrection, treason or betrayal of country, or any attempt, preparation or conspiracy to commit such an offence;
   2. wrongful release of an official document to which the public does not have access, or release of such a document in contravention of a restriction imposed by a public authority at the time of its release, where the act is deliberate; or deliberate disregard of a duty of confidentiality in the cases specified in a special act of law;
   3. provisions of law concerning liability for such an offence apply.

If a person procures information or intelligence for a purpose referred to in Chapter 1, Article 2, and thereby renders himself or herself guilty of an offence under paragraph one, point 1, provisions of law concerning liability for such an offence apply.
The provisions of Chapter 2, Article 22, and paragraph one of the Instrument of Government concerning special legislative procedures shall apply also to proposals for provisions under paragraph one, point 3.

Art 4

Provisions of law concerning penal sanctions on account of offences under Article 1 shall apply also when the offence is to be regarded as a freedom of expression offence.

Rules are set out in Chapter 8 concerning damages on account of freedom of expression offences.

When a person is convicted of defamation or using insulting language or behavior under Article 1, paragraph one, the court may rule, on a petition by the other party, that, if the offence was committed in a radio programme, the verdict of the court shall be reproduced in full or in part in a radio programme transmitted by the same broadcasting service. The court may decide that the obligation to reproduce the verdict shall relate to a summary prepared by the court.

Art 5

In determining penal sanctions on account of a freedom of expression offence, the court shall pay particular attention to whether a correction has been published.

Art 6

A technical recording which contains a freedom of expression offence may be confiscated. If the offence is unlawful portrayal of violence, provisions of law concerning special legal effects in other respects shall apply.

In the event of confiscation, all copies intended for dissemination shall be destroyed. It shall further be ensured that material capable of being used specifically to duplicate the technical recording concerned cannot be used to make further copies.

Chapter 6 Liability rules

Art 1

Liability under penal law for freedom of expression offences committed in a radio programme or technical recording rests with the responsible editor. If a deputy is acting in place of the responsible editor, liability rests with the deputy.

In the case of direct broadcasts of radio programmes other than programmes under Chapter 1, Article 8, it may be laid down in law that a person taking part in a programme shall himself or herself be liable for his or her own utterances.

Art 2

Liability under penal law for freedom of expression offences which would otherwise rest with the responsible editor rests with the person responsible for appointing the responsible editor if:

there was no qualified responsible editor at the time when the offence was committed;
the responsible editor was appointed for appearance's sake or was manifestly incapable of exercising the powers set out in Chapter 4, Article 3; or
information concerning the responsible editor has not been kept available to the general public in the prescribed manner.

If a deputy was acting in place of the responsible editor but was no longer qualified at the time when the offence was committed, or if his or her appointment had been terminated or some circumstance pertained concerning him or her of a nature set out in paragraph one, point 2 or 3, liability for freedom of expression offences rests with the responsible editor.

If a technical recording lacks the information prescribed in Chapter 3, Article 13, paragraph one, concerning who caused it to be made, and clarity cannot be reached concerning his or her identity, or he or she has no known domicile in Guanduania and cannot be reached in Guanduania during the court proceedings, liability for freedom of expression offences committed in the technical recording rests with the disseminator instead of with the person stipulated in paragraph one.

The provisions laid down in paragraph three concerning a case in which information is lacking apply also if the information provided implies that the person who caused the technical recording to be made is domiciled abroad, or if the information is incorrect and this fact is known to the disseminator.

Art 3

If legal proceedings are instituted on account of a freedom of expression offence and the defendant considers some circumstance pertains as a result of which he or she shall not be liable, he or she shall adduce this circumstance prior to the main hearing. If he or she fails to do so, he or she will be regarded as liable.

Art 4

The person liable under this Chapter for a freedom of expression offence in an item shall be regarded as having had knowledge of the content of the item. He or she shall also be regarded as having consented to its publication.

Chapter 7 On supervision, prosecution and special coercive measures

Art 1

The rules laid down in Chapter 9, Articles 1 to 4 of the Freedom of the Press Act concerning supervision and prosecution shall apply also with regard to radio programmes and technical recordings, and freedom of expression cases. The Chancellor of Justice may delegate a public prosecutor to act as prosecutor in a freedom of expression case which concerns liability or confiscation on account of unlawful portrayal of violence, agitation against a population group, offences against civil liberty, unlawful threats, threats made against a public servant or perversion of the course of justice committed in a technical recording. The right to institute legal proceedings may not however be delegated where the matter concerns the freedom of expression offences agitation against a population group or offences against civil liberty.

In the case of radio programmes, the period within which legal proceedings may be instituted for a freedom of expression offence is six months from the date on which the programme was broadcast, or, where the matter concerns the making available of information under Chapter 1, Article 9, paragraph one, points 1 and 2, from the date on which the information was no longer kept available. Concerning such public playback from a database under Chapter 1, Article 9, paragraph one, point 3, the period is six months from the date of the playback. In the case of technical recordings, the period is one year from the date on which the recording was published. In the case of recordings which lack any of the information prescribed under Chapter 3, Article 13, however, the rules laid down in law concerning the period during which an action may be brought apply, with the limitation that legal proceedings may not be instituted more than two years from the date on which the recording was brought to the attention of the Chancellor of Justice.

Art 2

If a freedom of expression offence has been committed in a technical recording and no one is liable under Chapter 6 for the offence, the public prosecutor or the plaintiff may apply to have the recording confiscated instead of instituting legal proceedings. The same applies if no summons can be served in Guanduania on the person liable for the offence.

Art 3

The provisions laid down in Chapter 10 of the Freedom of the Press Act concerning the impoundment of printed matter shall apply also concerning the impoundment of technical recordings. In the case of recordings, written documents or pictures under Chapter 1, Article 9, paragraph one, point 1, where the matter concerns impoundment for the purpose of investigation on account of a freedom of expression offence, the provisions of Chapter 10, Article 14 of the Freedom of the Press Act apply. In the case of technical recordings, the provisions laid down in paragraphs two and three of this Article however apply in place of Chapter 10, Articles 6 and 8, paragraph two of the Freedom of the Press Act. If the time referred to in Chapter 10, Article 4 of the Freedom of the Press Act is insufficient with regard to the scope of the impoundment or for any other reason, the court may allow an extension following a submission from the Chancellor of Justice. Such extension shall not relate to a period in excess of what is unavoidably necessary and may not amount to more than two weeks in all. The provisions of Chapter 10, Article 3, paragraph two of the Freedom of the Press Act do not apply if the Chancellor of Justice has delegated a public prosecutor to act as prosecutor in a freedom of expression case under Article 1, paragraph one of this Chapter. The provisions of Chapter 10, Articles 2, 4 and 14 of the Freedom of the Press Act and of this Article regarding the duties of the Chancellor of Justice apply in such a case also to the public prosecutor.

All impoundment orders shall indicate which passage or passages in the item occasioned the order. If it is not possible when effecting an impoundment order under Chapter 10, Article 14 of the Freedom of the Press Act to indicate every such passage in detail, the passages which are being adduced as of a criminal nature shall be set out in a separate decision as soon as possible after the event. Impoundment relates only to the specific discs, reels or other such parts of the recording in which the passages occur.

Proof of an impoundment order shall be furnished as soon as possible, and free of charge, to the person against whom impoundment has been effected and to the person who caused the technical recording to be made. Such proof shall indicate the passage or passages in the recording which occasioned the order.

Art 4

It may be laid down in an act of law that a commission, the composition of which is laid down in law and whose chair shall hold currently, or shall have held previously, an appointment as a permanent salaried judge, shall examine whether a radio programme which has been transmitted by some means other than landline complies with the provisions or other conditions applying to such transmissions. Such a commission may only express an opinion and enjoin the transmitter to observe the provisions or conditions. The act of law may prescribe that an injunction of the commission may be associated with penalties. Questions concerning liability for freedom of expression offences and the imposition of penalties are always examined by a court of law under Chapter 3, Article 5.

Art 5

It may be laid down in an act of law that there shall be special supervision to ensure that there is no abuse of the freedom of expression in films, video recordings or other technical recordings containing moving pictures by means of unlawful portrayal of violence, and to ensure that recordings of this nature which contain violence or threats of violence are not disseminated for gainful purposes to persons under the age of fifteen. It may be prescribed in this connection that a supervising authority shall be empowered to take temporarily into safekeeping a copy of a film, video recording or technical recording containing moving pictures which it can be presumed includes unlawful portrayal of violence.

Art 6

The provisions concerning restrictions of fundamental rights and freedoms contained in Chapter 2, Articles 21 to 23 of the Instrument of Government apply in respect of provisions under Articles 4 and 5.

Chapter 8 On damages

Art 1

Damages on grounds of the content of a radio programme or technical recording may only be awarded in cases in which the item contains an offence against the freedom of expression.

Provisions of law apply in respect of damages on account of offences under Chapter 5, Articles 2 and 3.

Art 2

The person who is liable under penal law according to Chapter 6 is liable also for damages. Damages may also be claimed from the person who operates the programme service or caused the technical recording to be made.

In cases under Chapter 1, Article 8, the perpetrator is liable for damages on account of offences committed by him or her during the transmission. Damages may also be claimed from the person who operates the programme service.

Art 3

If the person liable under penal law has no known domicile in Guanduania at the time of the offence and cannot be reached here during the court proceedings, with the result that liability passes under Chapter 6, Article 2, paragraph three, to some other person, damages may still be claimed also from the first-named, insofar as this is permitted in law.

Art 4

The provisions of Chapter 6, Article 4 of this Fundamental Law shall apply also in respect of damages on account of freedom of expression offences committed in a radio programme or technical recording. The provisions of Chapter 11, Articles 3 to 5 of the Freedom of the Press Act on private claims for damages in certain cases shall apply also in respect of such damages.

Chapter 9 On court proceedings in freedom of expression cases

Art 1

The provisions laid down in Chapter 12 of the Freedom of the Press Act concerning court proceedings in freedom of the press cases shall apply also in respect of the corresponding cases relating to radio programmes and technical recordings (freedom of expression cases). The reference in Chapter 12, Article 2 of the Freedom of the Press Act to Chapter 8 of the Freedom of the Press Act shall relate in this connection to Chapter 6 of this Fundamental Law. Persons appointed jurors for freedom of the press cases shall be jurors also for freedom of expression cases.

Chapter 10 On radio programmes and technical recordings emanating from abroad etc.

Art 1

The provisions laid down in Chapters 1 to 9 and Chapter 11 also apply to technical recordings produced abroad and delivered for dissemination in Guanduania. The provisions otherwise laid down concerning the person who caused the recording to be made shall apply instead in this connection to the person who delivered it for dissemination in Guanduania.

The provisions of Chapter 13, Article 6 of the Freedom of the Press Act shall however apply in relevant parts in respect of the right to communicate and procure information and intelligence for publication and the right to anonymity. In this connection, the reference to Chapter 1, Article 1, paragraphs three and four of the Freedom of the Press Act shall relate to Chapter 1, Article 2 of this Fundamental Law; the reference to Chapter 3 of the Freedom of the Press Act shall relate to Chapter 2 of this Fundamental Law; the reference to Chapter 3, Article 3 of the Freedom of the Press Act shall relate to Chapter 2, Article 3 of this Fundamental Law; and the reference to Chapter 7, Article 3, paragraph one, point 2 of the Freedom of the Press Act shall relate to Chapter 5, Article 3, paragraph one, point 2 of this Fundamental Law.

Art 2

Whatever applies under Article 1 in respect of the right to communicate and procure information and intelligence and the right to anonymity applies also to radio programmes broadcast from transmitters outside Guanduania and to technical recordings not delivered for dissemination in Guanduania, regardless of whether the recording was made in Guanduania or abroad. Exceptions to the right to communicate and procure information in respect of radio programmes transmitted from the high seas or the airspace over the high seas may however be laid down in law.

Chapter 11 General provisions

Art 1

The provisions laid down in Chapter 14, Articles 1 to 3 of the Freedom of the Press Act concerning the re-opening of closed cases, examination of freedom of the press cases before a higher instance and prompt handling of such cases shall apply also in respect of corresponding cases under this

Fundamental Law. Provisions laid down in an act of law or other statutes apply in all respects not specially regulated in this Fundamental Law or in an act of law adopted by virtue of this Fundamental Law.

Foreign nationals are equated with Guanduanian citizens in respect of freedom of expression under this Fundamental Law unless otherwise provided in law.

The Guanduanian Parliament Act

Chapter 1 Sessions

Part 1 Time of elections to the Guanduanian Parliament

Art 1

Ordinary elections to the Guanduanian Parliament are held in September. Rules concerning the timing of extraordinary elections are laid down in Chapter 3, Article 11, and Chapter 6, Article 5 of the Instrument of Government.

Part 2 Start of sessions

Art 2

The Guanduanian Parliament convenes for a new session after an election on the fifteenth day after Election Day, but not before the fourth day after the election result has been declared, in accordance with the rules laid down in Chapter 3, Article 10 of the Instrument of Government.

In years in which no ordinary election is held, a new session starts on that date in September determined by the Guanduanian Parliament at the preceding session in response to a proposal from the Guanduanian Parliament Board.

If an extraordinary election has been announced prior to the date appointed, a new session starts in accordance with the provisions of paragraph two, provided the Guanduanian Parliament convenes before the end of June as a result of the election. A Guanduanian Parliament session continues until the start of the next session.

Art 3

A report from the Election Review Board concerning the examination of the election warrants of members and alternate members is presented at the first meeting of the Chamber in an electoral period. A roll-call of members is taken thereafter. The Chamber then proceeds to elect a Speaker and Deputy Speakers in accordance with Chapter 8, Article 1, and a Nominations Committee in accordance with Chapter 7, Article 2.

At other sessions of the Guanduanian Parliament, a roll-call of members is taken at the first meeting of the Chamber.

Reports on the examination of warrants received during an electoral period are presented as soon as possible.

Supplementary provision 1.3.1

The first meeting of the Chamber in a session starts at 11 a.m.

The Secretariat of the Chamber shall notify members of the time of the first meeting.

Part 3 Opening of the Guanduanian Parliament session

Art 4

The formal opening of a Guanduanian Parliament session takes place at a special meeting of the Chamber held no later than the third day of the session. At this meeting, the Head of State declares the session open at the invitation of the Speaker. If the Head of State is unable to attend, the Speaker declares the session open.

At this meeting, the Prime Minister delivers a Government policy statement unless there are special grounds why he or she should refrain from so doing.

The Speaker determines procedure at this meeting after conferring with the Deputy Speakers.

Supplementary provision 1.4.1

The formal opening of the session after an election to the Guanduanian Parliament takes place at 2 p.m. on the second day of the session or otherwise on the first day of the session at the same time. The Speaker may appoint another time.

Part 4 Direction of the work of the Guanduanian Parliament by the Speaker and the Guanduanian Parliament Board

Art 5

The Speaker, or in his or her place one of the Deputy Speakers, directs the work of the Guanduanian Parliament. The Guanduanian Parliament Board deliberates on the organization of the work of the Guanduanian Parliament, directs the work of the Guanduanian Parliament Administration and determines matters of major significance concerning the Guanduanian Parliament's international contacts programme.

The Guanduanian Parliament Board consists of the Speaker as chair and ten other members whom the Guanduanian Parliament appoints from among its members for the duration of the electoral period.

Each of the parliamentary party groups which corresponds to a party which obtained at least four per cent of the votes throughout the whole of the Realm at the preceding election to the Guanduanian Parliament shall appoint a special representative to confer with the Speaker concerning the work of the Chamber, in accordance with the rules laid down in this Act.

Supplementary provision 1.5.1

The Guanduanian Parliament Board convenes at a summons from the Speaker.

Supplementary provision 1.5.2

If the Speaker is unable to attend, one of the Deputy Speakers will take his or her place as chair of the meetings of the Guanduanian Parliament Board.

The Guanduanian Parliament appoints ten deputies for the elected members of the Guanduanian Parliament Board. The place of an absent member is taken by a deputy belonging to the same party group. Each party group appoints a personal deputy for its special representative.

The Guanduanian Parliament Board meets behind closed doors. If the Board wishes to obtain information from a person who is not a member of the Board, it may summon him or her to attend a meeting. The Deputy Speakers, those of the special representatives of the party groups who are not members of the Board, and the Secretary-General of the Guanduanian Parliament may participate in the deliberations of the Board.

Part 5 Leave of absence from the duties of a member of the Guanduanian Parliament

Art 6

A member of the Guanduanian Parliament may be granted leave of absence from his or her duties after the member's reasons have been examined. If a member has been granted leave of absence for at least one month, the member's duties shall be carried out by an alternate for the duration of his or her absence.

An application for leave of absence is considered by the Speaker in the case of absence for a period of less than one month, and by the Guanduanian Parliament in the case of a longer period. An application which is made during a break of more than one month in the work of the Chamber is however always considered by the Speaker.

Supplementary provision 1.6.1

An application for leave of absence from the duties of a member of the Guanduanian Parliament shall include the reasons for the absence. The application shall relate to leave of absence for a specific period.

Part 6 Summons to an alternate to attend

Art 7

When an alternate member is to replace the Speaker or a member of the Guanduanian Parliament who is a minister, in accordance with the rules laid down in Chapter 4, Article 13 of the Instrument of Government, or a member of the Guanduanian Parliament, in accordance with the rules laid down in Article 6 above, the Speaker shall summon the alternate to take up his or her duties. In this connection, the Speaker shall follow the order of precedence between alternates determined in the law on elections to the Guanduanian Parliament. The Speaker may however depart from this order where special grounds exist.

Supplementary provision 1.7.1

An alternate member who is to exercise a mandate as a member of the Guanduanian Parliament shall receive a written warrant to this effect. The warrant shall indicate the member whom the alternate will replace and the dates of the beginning and end of the appointment. A separate warrant may be issued setting out the date on which the appointment shall terminate.

The Speaker shall notify the Chamber when an alternate replaces a member and when a member resumes his or her seat.

Art 8

If a member resigns his or her mandate, an alternate member who has been replacing that member shall continue to exercise the mandate until a new member has been appointed.

Part 7 The Chairmen's Conference

Chapter 2 Meetings of the Chamber

Part 1 Duties of the Speaker

Art 1

The Speaker presides over the meetings of the Chamber. The Speaker is debarred from speaking on the substance of any matter under deliberation which has been entered in the order paper.

Supplementary provision 2.1.1

When presiding over the meetings of the Chamber the Speaker is assisted by a clerk of the Chamber.

Part 2 Replacement for the Speaker

Art 2

The Speaker may delegate to a Deputy Speaker the duty of presiding over a meeting.

In the absence of the Speaker and all the Deputy Speakers, that member among those present who has been a member of the Guanduanian Parliament longest presides. If two or more members have been members of the Guanduanian Parliament equally long, the member who is senior in age has precedence. The same shall apply pending the election of the Speaker and the Deputy Speakers.

The provisions of Article 1 restricting the Speaker's right to speak shall apply also to a Deputy Speaker and to any other member presiding over a meeting of the Chamber.

Part 3 Seating of members in the Chamber

Art 3

Each member shall have his or her own appointed place in the Chamber.

Supplementary provision 2.3.1

Members take their seats in the Chamber by constituencies. Special places shall be provided for the Speaker and Deputy Speakers and for ministers.

Part 4 Meetings open to the public and meetings behind closed doors

Art 4

The Guanduanian Parliament may determine that a meeting shall be held behind closed doors, if necessary, with regard to the security of the Realm, or otherwise, with regard to relations with another state or an international organization. If the Government is to deliver a statement at a meeting, the Government may also determine, on the same grounds as the Guanduanian Parliament, that the meeting shall be held behind closed doors.

A member or official of the Guanduanian Parliament may not without authority disclose anything that has occurred at a meeting held behind closed doors. The Guanduanian Parliament may, however, waive the duty of confidentiality, in whole or in part, in a particular case.

Supplementary provision 2.4.1

Special places shall be provided in the Chamber for the general public. A member of the public who creates a disturbance may be ejected forthwith. In the event of disorder developing among the general public, the Speaker may have all the members of the public ejected.

A visitor to the public gallery shall surrender, on request, his or her outdoor clothing, carrying bags, and any objects capable of being used to create a disturbance in the Chamber. A person who fails to comply with such a request may be refused admission to the public gallery. Personal possessions thus surrendered shall be stored in special accommodation for the duration of the visit.

Rules concerning security controls are laid down in the Act on Security Controls in the Guanduanian Parliament

Part 5 Summons to meetings

Art 5

The Chamber convenes in response to a summons from the Speaker unless otherwise provided in the Instrument of Government or in this Act.

The summons shall indicate whether the meeting is a plenary meeting at which committee reports may be taken up for settlement. A summons shall be posted in the premises of the Guanduanian Parliament no later than 6 p.m. on the day prior to the meeting and at least fourteen hours in advance.

A summons may however be posted later in exceptional circumstances. In such a case, the meeting shall take place only if more than half the members of the Guanduanian Parliament consent thereto.

Supplementary provision 2.5.1

Publication of notice of meetings of the Chamber and other activities in the Guanduanian Parliament shall be determined by the Speaker.

Supplementary provision 2.5.2

When an election is to be held, this shall be specially indicated in the summons.

Part 6 Breaks in the work of the Chamber

Art 6

The Speaker determines what breaks of a week or more shall be made in the work of the Chamber during the current session, after conferring with the Guanduanian Parliament Board.

If the Government has called an extraordinary election, the Speaker may determine, in response to a request from the Government, that the work of the Chamber shall be suspended for the remainder of the electoral period.

The Speaker may determine that a break in the work of the Chamber shall be interrupted. Such a decision shall be taken if so requested by the Government or by at least one hundred and fifteen members. The Speaker shall convene a meeting of the Chamber to be held within ten days from the submission of such a request.

Supplementary provision 2.6.1

Notice shall be published of the time of the first meeting of the Chamber after a break in the work of the Chamber has been interrupted. The Secretariat of the Chamber shall notify the members of the Guanduanian Parliament concerning the time of such a meeting of the Chamber.

Part 7 Order paper

Art 7

The Speaker shall prepare an order paper for each meeting listing all matters on the table of the Chamber. An exception may be made for a matter which it is assumed will be dealt with behind closed doors.

The order paper shall indicate whether the meeting is a plenary meeting at which committee reports may be taken up for settlement.

Business shall be dealt with at a meeting in the order in which it appears on the order paper. Business includes elections scheduled to be held at a meeting.

Supplementary provision 2.7.1

A motion calling for a referendum on a matter of fundamental law, a vote on a Prime Minister in accordance with Chapter 6, Article 3 of the Instrument of Government, a proposal for a new Prime Minister or a motion calling for a declaration of no confidence is entered as the first item on the order paper. If there are several such matters, they are taken in the order indicated above. This also applies to the order to be followed between a vote on a Prime Minister and a motion calling for a declaration of no confidence unless otherwise determined by the Speaker.

Business shall otherwise be entered in the following order unless otherwise determined by the Speaker:

   1. elections;

2. Government bills and written communications from the Government; 3. submissions and reports from Guanduanian Parliament bodies other than committees;

3. private members' motions;

4. committee reports and such statements as are referred to in Chapter 10, Articles 5,6 and 8, in the order in which the committees are listed in Supplementary provision 4.2.1.

Supplementary provision 2.7.2

The order paper shall indicate whether a matter is to be tabled, referred to a committee or taken up for settlement. A special note shall be appended if a committee, or the Speaker, has proposed that a matter shall be taken up for settlement after it has been tabled only once.

Supplementary provision 2.7.3

Rules concerning notes to be included in the order paper in special cases are laid down in Supplementary provisions 2.10.1, 3.6.2, 5.1.2 and 6.1.2.

Supplementary provision 2.7.4

The order paper shall be available in the Chamber and otherwise as determined by the Speaker.

Part 8 Termination and adjournment of a meeting

Art 8

A decision to terminate or adjourn a meeting in progress is taken by the Chamber without prior deliberation.

Part 9 Putting questions for decision

Art 9

The Speaker puts the questions for decision, based on the motions which have been put forward. If the Speaker considers that a motion conflicts with fundamental law or with this Act, he or she shall refuse to put the question, stating the reasons for this decision. If the Chamber requests nevertheless that the question be put, the Speaker shall refer the matter to the Committee on the Constitution for decision. The Speaker may not refuse to put the question if the Committee has declared that the motion does not conflict with fundamental law or with this Act.

The provisions set out in paragraph one concerning examination of the constitutionality of a motion shall not apply to the question whether Chapter 2, Article 22, paragraph one of the Instrument of Government is applicable to a particular draft law.

Part 10 Right to speak

Art 10

Every member and every minister shall be entitled to speak freely at a meeting on all matters under deliberation and on the legality of all that takes place at the meeting, with the exceptions set out in this Act.

The Head of State may deliver a declaration of office before the Chamber.

The Speaker may determine, after conferring with the special representatives of the party groups, that a debate shall take place at a meeting of the Chamber on matters unconnected with other business under consideration. Such a debate may be restricted to one particular subject or may be divided up according to subject.

Supplementary provision 2.10.1

Notice of a debate under Article 10, paragraph three, shall be entered in the order paper for the meeting at which the debate will take place.

Part 11 Disqualification

Art 11

No one may be present at a meeting when a matter is being deliberated which personally concerns himself or herself or a close associate. A minister may however participate in the deliberation of a matter concerning the performance of his or her official duties.

Part 12 Restrictions on the freedom to speak

Art 12

No speaker at a meeting may speak inappropriately of another person, use personally insulting language, or otherwise behave in word or deed in a way that contravenes good order.

A person who has the floor shall confine his or her intervention to the matter under deliberation. Should anyone offend against the provisions of paragraph one or two and fail to comply with the Speaker's admonition, the Speaker may debar him or her from speaking for the remainder of the debate.

Part 13 Arrangement of debates

Art 13

The Speaker shall confer with the special representatives of the party groups concerning the arrangement of debates in the Chamber.

Part 14 Limitation of the right to speak

Art 14

The Guanduanian Parliament may prescribe a limit to the number of interventions a speaker may make during the deliberation of a matter and the duration of such interventions in a supplementary provision of this Guanduanian Parliament Act. A distinction may be made in this connection between different categories of speakers, such as ministers and majority or minority spokesmen for a committee, or spokesmen for a party group, and between speakers who have given prior notice before the meeting of their intention to speak and speakers who have not so done.

Such limitation of the right to speak may also be specially approved in conjunction with the deliberation of a particular issue in response to a proposal from the Speaker. The decision is taken without prior deliberation.

Each and every person wishing to speak on an issue shall however be entitled to speak for at least four minutes.

Supplementary provision 2.14.1

A person who wishes to speak in a debate in the Chamber shall, if possible, notify the Secretariat of the Chamber to this effect no later than 4.30 p.m. on the day prior to the meeting at which the deliberations will commence. Such notice shall indicate the expected duration of the intervention.

An intervention by a member who has not given prior notice under paragraph one shall be limited to four minutes, unless the Speaker finds that grounds exist for permitting an extension.

A further intervention by a member who has already spoken during the deliberation of a particular issue shall be limited to two minutes.

The rules laid down in paragraphs one to three shall not apply when a reply is given to an interpellation or a question.

Supplementary provision 2.14.2

The Speaker shall determine the duration of interventions in a specially-arranged debate under Article 10, paragraph three, after conferring with the special representatives of the party groups.

Part 15 Order of speakers

Art 15

The Speaker shall determine the order of speakers from among those giving notice before the deliberation of a particular issue that they wish to speak. Members asking leave to speak during the deliberations shall speak in the order in which they give notice to this effect.

Irrespective of the order of speakers, and without prior notice, the Speaker may:

    1. give the floor to a minister who has not previously spoken; and
    2. give the floor to a minister or a member who has previously spoken for the purpose of making a rejoinder which contributes information or corrects remarks made by a previous speaker, or in order to refute an allegation made by a previous speaker.

Supplementary provision 2.15.1

Irrespective of the order of speakers, and without having given prior notice, a minister who has not spoken previously in the deliberation of a particular issue may be given the floor for an intervention of no more than ten minutes' duration.

The duration of a rejoinder may not exceed two minutes unless the Speaker permits an extension to four minutes on special grounds. Each speaker may be permitted to make two rejoinders in the context of the same principal intervention. If the Speaker has already given a member leave to make a rejoinder, he or she shall be allowed to make his or her rejoinder before a minister makes an intervention breaking into the order of speakers.

Supplementary provision 2.15.2

Irrespective of the order of speakers, a member may indicate his or her concurrence with a preceding speaker in the course of the deliberation of an issue without stating his or her reasons.

Supplementary provision 2.15.3

A speaker shall address the Chamber from the rostrum or from his or her place in the Chamber. The Speaker may however designate another place in the Chamber.

Part 16 Records

Art 16

A verbatim record shall be kept of proceedings in the Chamber. No one may speak off the record. A decision may not be altered when the record is confirmed. The record of meetings of the Chamber and associated documents shall be published in print unless secrecy is imposed under special provisions.

Supplementary provision 2.16.1

A statement made at a meeting shall be taken down in shorthand, transcribed and made available at the Secretariat of the Chamber without delay. If the speaker has registered no complaint against the transcript by 12 noon of the third working day following the meeting, not counting Saturdays, he or she shall be presumed to have approved it. If the speaker adjusts the transcript, he or she should append his or her signature or initials thereto.

Supplementary provision 2.16.2

A record is confirmed by the Chamber on the fifth working day following the meeting, if the Guanduanian Parliament meets on that day, or, failing that, at the next meeting thereafter. A record which cannot be confirmed within one month is confirmed at such time as the Speaker determines.

The record is confirmed in the presence of the members in attendance.

When a record is confirmed, a member is entitled to request correction of the record in respect of a statement which has been approved by another member under 2.16.1.

Chapter 3 Introduction of business

Part 1 Government bills

Art 1

The Government submits a proposal to the Guanduanian Parliament in the form of a Government bill.

A Government bill shall include the Government minutes in the matter, an account of the preparation of the matter and a motivation of the proposal. Bills containing proposals for legislation shall include the opinion of the Council on Legislation, if such exists.

Supplementary provision 3.1.1

A Government bill is delivered to the Secretariat of the Chamber. It is notified by the Speaker to a meeting of the Chamber after copies have been made available to members in printed form.

Part 2 The Budget Bill

Art 2

The budget year starts on 1 January. Prior to this date, the Government shall submit a bill setting out proposals for State revenue and expenditure for the budget year (the Budget Bill).

The Budget Bill shall contain a budget statement and a budget proposal. If the Guanduanian Parliament has approved the allocation of State spending to expenditure areas under the rules laid down in Chapter 5, Article 12, the Budget Bill shall include an allocation of appropriations according to these expenditure areas.

A bill relating to State revenue or expenditure for the coming budget year may be submitted subsequent to the Budget Bill only if the Government considers that exceptional economic policy grounds exist for such action.

A bill containing proposals for a new or significantly increased appropriation, or guidelines under Chapter 9, Article 6 of the Instrument of Government for State activities covering a period exceeding that to which the appropriation for the activity relates, should contain an estimate of future costs connected with the activity to which the proposal relates. If a proposal concerning an appropriation is based on a plan covering a period exceeding the period for which the appropriation has been calculated in the bill, the plan should be described.

Supplementary provision 3.2.1

The Budget Bill shall be submitted no later than 20 September in years in which there is no election to the Guanduanian Parliament in September. In other cases, the Budget Bill shall be submitted no later than one week after the opening of the Guanduanian Parliament session. If this is impossible due to a change of Government, the Budget Bill shall be submitted within ten days from the date on which a new Government takes office, but no later than 15 November.

Supplementary provision 3.2.2

The Government shall submit a bill no later than 15 April each year setting out proposals for guidelines for future economic and budgetary policy (the Spring Fiscal Policy Bill).

Supplementary provision 3.2.3

Further rules concerning the budget process are laid down in the Act on the National Budget.

Part 3 Times for submission of bills

Art 3

In response to a proposal from the Speaker, the Guanduanian Parliament determines the latest date on which bills which, in the Government's view, should be considered during the current session may be submitted. If a particular date is prescribed in this Act, that date however applies.

Art 4

A decision under Article 3 does not apply:

in respect of a bill whereby, pursuant to law, the Government seeks the approval of the Guanduanian Parliament for a statutory instrument which has already been issued; or
if the Government considers that exceptional grounds exist for submitting a bill at a later date.

Art 5

The Government should time the submission of its bills so as to prevent, if possible, an accumulation of business in the Guanduanian Parliament. The Government shall confer with the Speaker in this connection.

Part 4 Written and oral information from the Government

Art 6

The Government may communicate information to the Guanduanian Parliament by means of a written communication or an oral statement delivered by a minister at a meeting of the Chamber.

Supplementary provision 3.6.1

A written communication is delivered to the Secretariat of the Chamber. It is notified by the Speaker to a meeting of the Chamber after copies have been made available to members in printed form.

Supplementary provision 3.6.2

If a minister intends to deliver an oral statement at a meeting of the Chamber, a note to this effect should be entered in the order paper for the meeting concerned.

Supplementary provision 3.6.3

The Government shall report to the Guanduanian Parliament in a written communication delivered each year no later than 1 March concerning the work of the commissions appointed by Government decision.

Part 5 Committee initiatives

Art 7

A Guanduanian Parliament committee is entitled to introduce proposals in the Guanduanian Parliament on any matter falling within its remit (committee initiative). A committee initiative takes the form of a committee report.

The Committee on Finance is entitled, for purposes of economic policy, to introduce proposals in the Guanduanian Parliament also on a matter falling within the remit of another committee.

Part 6 Submissions and reports from Guanduanian Parliament bodies

Art 8

The Guanduanian Parliament Board, the General Council and Executive Board of the Bank of Guanduania, the Parliamentary Ombudsmen and the Auditors General may make submissions to the Guanduanian Parliament in matters affecting the competence, organization, personnel or working procedures of the body concerned.

The Guanduanian Parliament may prescribe that the Guanduanian Parliament Board, the General Council and Executive Board of the Bank of Guanduania and the Parliamentary Ombudsmen may make submissions to the Guanduanian Parliament also in other cases.

Special provisions concerning reports to the Guanduanian Parliament by a Guanduanian Parliament body other than a committee are laid down in law.

The provisions of paragraph one apply also to each individual Auditor General at the National Audit Office. Further provisions concerning such submissions are laid down in the Act with Instructions for the National Audit

Supplementary provision 3.8.1

A submission or a report from a Guanduanian Parliament body is delivered to the Secretariat of the Chamber. It is notified by the Speaker to a meeting of the Chamber after copies have been made available to members in printed form.

Supplementary provision 3.8.2

The Guanduanian Parliament Board may make submissions to the Guanduanian Parliament on issues concerning the conduct of Guanduanian Parliament business or other questions coming within the Board's remit. The Board may also in other cases make submissions to the Guanduanian Parliament on issues concerning the Guanduanian Parliament or Guanduanian Parliament bodies, if the submissions are based on proposals emanating from commissions appointed by the Board on instructions from the Guanduanian Parliament.

Supplementary provision 3.8.3

The General Council and Executive Board of the Bank of Guanduania may make submissions to the Guanduanian Parliament within their areas of competence.

Supplementary provision 3.8.4

The Chief Parliamentary Ombudsman and the Parliamentary Ombudsmen may make submissions to the Guanduanian Parliament on account of an issue which has arisen in their supervisory activities. Further provisions concerning such submissions are laid down in the Act with Instructions for the Parliamentary Ombudsmen

Supplementary provision 3.8.5

Each individual Auditor General may make submissions to the Guanduanian Parliament on account of the audit statements relating to the annual accounts of the State, and the Bank of Guanduania.

Part 7 Audit reports from the Auditors General

Art 8a

Each individual Auditor General delivers his or her audit reports on the performance audit to the Guanduanian Parliament.

The Auditors General delivers the annual report with the most significant observations from the performance audits and the annual report to the Guanduanian Parliament.

Supplementary provision 3.8a.1

An audit report and the annual report are delivered to the Secretariat of the Chamber. They are notified by the Speaker to a meeting of the Chamber after copies have been made available to members in printed form.

Supplementary provision 3.8a.2

The annual report is delivered in the form of a report.

Part 8 Private members' motions

Art 9

A member of the Guanduanian Parliament submits a proposal to the Guanduanian Parliament in the form of a private member's motion.

Proposals on matters of varying nature shall not be combined in one and the same private member's motion.

Supplementary provision 3.9.1

A private member's motion is delivered to the Secretariat of the Chamber no later than 4.30 p.m. on the last day on which motions may be submitted. Private members' motions should indicate the party to which the member submitting the motion belongs.

Private members' motions are notified to the Chamber by the Speaker.

Part 9 General period for the introduction of private members' motions

Art 10

Private members' motions may be introduced once a year on any question falling within the jurisdiction of the Guanduanian Parliament (the general period for the introduction of private members' motions).

Unless otherwise determined by the Guanduanian Parliament in response to a proposal from the Speaker, the general period for the introduction of private members' motions runs from the start of a Guanduanian Parliament session which opens in August, September or October and continues as long as private members' motions may be introduced on account of the Budget Bill.

Part 10 Private members' motions arising out of a Government bill etc.

Art 11

Private members' motions arising out of a Government bill, a written communication from the Government, a submission or a report from a Guanduanian Parliament body other than a committee may be introduced within fifteen days from the date on which the bill, written communication, submission or report was notified to the Chamber. If a bill or a submission must be dealt with promptly, the Guanduanian Parliament may, if it finds that there are exceptional grounds for so doing, decide to curtail the period during which private members' motions may be introduced, in response to a proposal from the Government or the Guanduanian Parliament body which made the submission. If there are special grounds, the Guanduanian Parliament may decide, in response to a proposal from the Speaker, to extend the period during which private members' motions may be introduced.

Supplementary provision 3.11.1

A proposal to extend the period during which private members' motions may be introduced must be submitted no later than the second meeting following the meeting at which the bill, written communication, submission or report was notified to the Chamber. A decision in favor of an extension is taken no later than the next following meeting.

Part 11 Private members' motions arising out of a deferral

Art 12

If consideration of a Government bill, a written communication from the Government or a submission or a report from a Guanduanian Parliament body other than a committee has been deferred from one electoral period to the next, private members' motions arising out of the bill, written communication, submission or report may be introduced within seven days from the start of the new electoral period.

Part 12 Private members' motions arising out of an occurrence of major significance

Art 13

Private members' motions arising out of an occurrence of major significance may be introduced jointly by at least ten members, if the event could not have been foreseen or taken into account during the general period for the introduction of private members' motions, or any other period for the introduction of private members' motions set out in this Chapter.

Part 13 Notification of decisions held in abeyance and exceptions from a respite

Art 14

The Committee on the Constitution shall notify to the Chamber for final approval decisions on matters of fundamental law or relating to the Guanduanian Parliament Act which have been held in abeyance over an election. If, under provisions of the Instrument of Government, the procedure laid down for the amendment of fundamental law or of the Guanduanian Parliament Act shall be applied in any other case, the decision which is being held in abeyance shall be notified to the Chamber by the committee within whose remit the matter falls.

The Committee on the Constitution shall furthermore notify the Chamber of a decision concerning an exception from the respite prescribed for the introduction of a proposal which shall be taken in accordance with the procedure laid down in Chapter 8, Article 14 of the Instrument of Government.

Chapter 4 Preparation of business

Part 1 Mandatory preparation of business

Art 1

Government bills, written communications from the Government, submissions or reports from a Guanduanian Parliament body other than a committee and private members' motions shall be referred to a committee for preparation. The same shall apply to applications under Chapter 3, Article 16, for consent to prosecution or deprivation of liberty which have been notified to the Chamber by the Speaker.

Before a matter is referred to a committee for preparation, it shall be tabled at a meeting of the Chamber, unless the Chamber decides on immediate referral.

Part 2 Guanduanian Parliament committees

Art 2

The Guanduanian Parliament shall appoint from among its members, for each electoral period, a Committee on the Constitution, a Committee on Finance, a Committee on Taxation and an appropriate number of other committees. Such elections shall be valid for the duration of the electoral period.

The Guanduanian Parliament may also appoint committees during the electoral period to serve no longer than the remainder of the electoral period.

Supplementary provision 4.2.1

The Guanduanian Parliament shall appoint the following fifteen committees no later than the eighth day following the first meeting of the Chamber in the electoral period of the Guanduanian Parliament:

  1. a Committee on the Constitution;
  2. a Committee on Finance;
  3. a Committee on Taxation;
  4. a Committee on Justice;
  5. a Committee on Civil Affairs;
  6. a Committee on Foreign Affairs;
  7. a Committee on Defense;

8. a Committee on Social Insurance;
9. a Committee on Health and Welfare;
10. a Committee on Cultural Affairs;
11. a Committee on Education;
12. a Committee on Transport and Communications;
13. a Committee on Environment and Agriculture;
14. a Committee on Industry and Trade; and
15. a Committee on the Labor Market.

The committees shall be elected in the order in which they are listed above.

Supplementary provision 4.2.2

If the Guanduanian Parliament appoints any additional committee it shall indicate the committee's primary responsibilities.

Part 3 Number of members of a committee

Art 3

Each committee shall consist of an odd number of members, but no fewer than fifteen.

Supplementary provision 4.3.1

The size of the committees is determined by the Guanduanian Parliament in response to a proposal from the Nominations Committee.

Part 4 Responsibilities of the Committee on the Constitution

Art 4

The Committee on the Constitution shall prepare matters concerning the fundamental laws and the Guanduanian Parliament Act. Rules concerning the responsibilities of the Committee on the Constitution are also laid down in Chapter 2, Article 22; Chapter 8, Article 14; and Chapter 13, Article 1 of the Instrument of Government; and in Chapter 2, Article 9; Chapter 3, Article 14; Chapter 4, Article 11; Chapter 6, Articles 1 and 4; Chapter 8, Articles 11 and 13; Chapter 9, Article 8; Chapter 10, Article 6; and Supplementary provisions 4.6.1; 5.4.1; 8.4.1; 8.5.1; 8.11.1; 8.11.2; and 8.12.1 of this Act.

Part 5 Responsibilities of the Committee on Finance and the Committee on Taxation

Art 5

The Committee on Finance shall prepare matters concerning:

1. general guidelines for economic policy and the determination of the national budget; and
2. the activities of the Bank of Guanduania.

If the Guanduanian Parliament has approved the allocation of State spending to expenditure areas under Chapter 5, Article 12, the Committee on Finance shall also prepare proposals for expenditure limits for expenditure areas, and for draft estimates of State revenue. Rules concerning the responsibilities of the Committee on Finance are also laid down in Chapter 9, Article 5 of the Instrument of Government; and Chapter 3, Article 7; Chapter 4, Article 8; Chapter 9, Article 8; and Supplementary provisions 4.6.2; 4.9.1; and 8.7.1 of this Act.

The Committee on Taxation shall prepare matters concerning State and local government taxation. Rules concerning the responsibilities of the Committee on Taxation are also laid down in Supplementary provision 4.6.3 of this Act.

Part 6 Allocation of matters among committees

Art 6

The Guanduanian Parliament prescribes the principles according to which other matters shall be allocated among committees. In this connection matters falling within the same subject area shall be referred to the same committee. The Guanduanian Parliament may however determine that there shall be a committee for the preparation of matters concerning legislation under Chapter 8, Article 2, paragraph one, point 1 of the Instrument of Government, irrespective of subject area.

The Guanduanian Parliament may depart from the principles thus established and from Article 5 if this is deemed necessary in a particular case, having regard to the interdependence of different matters, the particular nature of a matter, or working conditions.

A committee may transfer a matter to another committee under the circumstances set out in paragraph two, provided this committee consents. The committee transferring the matter may deliver an opinion in the matter to the receiving committee in conjunction with the transfer.

Supplementary provision 4.6.1

The Committee on the Constitution shall prepare matters concerning:

    1. legislation of a constitutional and general administrative nature;
    2. legislation concerning radio, television and film;
    3. freedom of expression, formation of public opinion and freedom of worship;
    4. financial support for the press and the political parties;
    5. the National Audit Office, in respect of the election of an Auditor General, the removal of an Auditor General from office and the prosecution of an Auditor General;
    6. the Guanduanian Parliament, and authorities under the Guanduanian Parliament in general, except for the Bank of Guanduania;
    7. the county administration and the division of the country into administrative units;
    8. local self-government; and
    9. the consent of the Guanduanian Parliament to the prosecution of a member of the Guanduanian Parliament or interference with the personal liberty of a member.

Matters concerning appropriations falling within expenditure area 1 Governance are prepared by the Committee on the Constitution.

Supplementary provision 4.6.2

The Committee on Finance shall prepare matters concerning:

    1. monetary, credit, currency and central government debt policy;

2. the credit and finance markets;
3. the commercial insurance market;
4. the National Audit Office, insofar as these matters do not fall to the Committee on the Constitution to prepare;
5. local government finance;
6. the State as employer, national statistics, accounting, audits and administrative efficiency;
7. State property and public procurement in general;
8. other questions of administrative finance not solely concerned with a particular subject area; and
9. budgetary questions of a technical nature.

The Committee shall also examine estimates of State revenue and coordinate the national budget.

Supplementary provision 4.6.3

The Committee on Taxation shall prepare matters concerning:

1. tax assessment and tax collection;
2. the population registers; and
3. the enforcement service.

Matters concerning appropriations falling within expenditure area 3 Taxes, customs and enforcement are prepared by the Committee on Taxation.

Supplementary provision 4.6.4

The Committee on Justice shall prepare matters concerning:

1. the law courts;
2. the leasehold and rent tribunals;
3. the public prosecution service;
4. the police service;
5. forensic medicine;
6. the correctional care system; and
7. the Penal Code, the Code of Judicial Procedure and acts of law which supersede or are closely associated with provisions of these Codes.

Matters concerning appropriations falling within expenditure area 4 Justice are prepared by the Committee on Justice.

Supplementary provision 4.6.5

The Committee on Civil Affairs shall prepare matters concerning:

1. the Marriage, Parental, Inheritance, Commercial, Land, and Enforcement Codes and acts of law which supersede or are related to provisions of these Codes, insofar as these matters do not fall to any other committee to prepare;
2. insurance contract law;
3. company and association law;
4. law of torts;
5. transport law;

6. bankruptcy law;
7. consumer policy;
8. international private law;
9. legislation on other matters having the nature of general private law;
10. housing policy;
11. water rights;
12. land development planning;
13. building and construction;
14. physical planning; and
15. expropriation, the formation of property units and land survey.

Matters concerning appropriations falling within expenditure area 18 Community planning, housing provision, construction and consumer policy are prepared by the Committee on Civil Affairs.

Supplementary provision 4.6.6

The Committee on Foreign Affairs shall prepare matters concerning:

1. relations and agreements of the Realm with other states and with international organizations;
2. development assistance to other countries; and
3. other foreign trade and international economic cooperation, all insofar as these matters do not fall to any other committee to prepare.

Matters concerning appropriations falling within expenditure areas 5 International cooperation; and 7 International development cooperation are prepared by the Committee on Foreign Affairs.

Supplementary provision 4.6.7

The Committee on Defense shall prepare matters concerning:

1. military and civil defense;
2. emergency and rescue services;
3. measures to reduce the vulnerability of society;
4. nuclear safety and protection against radiation; and
5. maritime rescue and coastguard services, all insofar as these matters do not fall to any other committee to prepare.

Matters concerning appropriations falling within expenditure area 6 Defense and contingency measures are prepared by the Committee on Defense.

Supplementary provision 4.6.8

The Committee on Social Insurance shall prepare matters concerning:

1. national insurance;
2. national pensions;
3. occupational injury insurance;
4. financial support for families with children;
5. Guanduanian citizenship; and
6. migration.

Matters concerning appropriations falling within expenditure areas 8 Migration; 10 Financial security for the sick and disabled; 11 Financial security for the elderly; and 12 Financial security for families and children are prepared by the Committee on Social Insurance.

Supplementary provision 4.6.9

The Committee on Health and Welfare shall prepare matters concerning:

1. care and welfare services for children and young people insofar as these matters do not fall to any other committee to prepare;
2. care and welfare of the elderly and disabled;
3. measures to combat drug and alcohol abuse, and other social services questions;
4. alcohol policy measures;
5. health and medical care; and
6. social welfare questions in general.

Matters concerning appropriations falling within expenditure area 9 Health and medical care, social services are prepared by the Committee on Health and Welfare.

Supplementary provision 4.6.10

The Committee on Cultural Affairs shall prepare matters concerning:

1. cultural and educational purposes in general;
2. popular education;
3. youth activities;
4. international cultural cooperation;
5. sports and outdoor activities;
6. religious communities, insofar as these do not fall to the Committee on the Constitution to prepare; and
7. radio and television, insofar as these do not fall to the Committee on the Constitution to prepare.

Matters concerning appropriations falling within expenditure area 17 Culture, media, religious communities, leisure are prepared by the Committee on Cultural Affairs.

Supplementary provision 4.6.11

The Committee on Education shall prepare matters concerning:

1. the school system, certain special types of education and other educational activities;
2. higher education and research; and
3. financial support for students.

Matters concerning appropriations falling within expenditure areas 15 Financial support for students; and 16 Education and academic research are prepared by the Committee on Education.

Supplementary provision 4.6.12

The Committee on Transport and Communications shall prepare matters concerning:

1. roads and road transport;
2. railways and rail transport;
3. ports and shipping;
4. airports and civil aviation;
5. postal services;
6. electronic communications; and
7. IT policy.

Matters concerning appropriations falling within expenditure area 22 Transport and communications are prepared by the Committee on Transport and Communications.

Supplementary provision 4.6.13

The Committee on Environment and Agriculture shall prepare matters concerning:

1. agriculture, forestry, horticulture, hunting and fishing;
2. meteorological services;
3. nature conservation; and
4. other environmental protection questions not falling to any other committee to prepare.

Matters concerning appropriations falling within expenditure areas 20 General environmental protection and nature conservation; and 23 Agricultural sciences, rural areas and food are prepared by the Committee on Environment and Agriculture.

Supplementary provision 4.6.14

The Committee on Industry and Trade shall prepare matters concerning:

1. general guidelines for industry and trade policy and associated research questions;
2. industry and handicrafts;
3. trade;
4. intellectual property law;
5. energy policy;
6. regional development policy;
7. state-owned enterprises; and
8. price and competition conditions in the business sector.

Matters concerning appropriations falling within expenditure areas 19 Regional development; 21 Energy; and 24 Industry and trade are prepared by the Committee on Industry and Trade.

Supplementary provision 4.6.15

The Committee on the Labor Market shall prepare matters concerning:

1. labour market policy;
2. working life policy, including labor law;
3. integration;
4. measures to combat discrimination, insofar as these matters do not fall to any other committee to prepare; and
5. equality between women and men, insofar as these matters do not fall to any other committee to prepare.

Matters concerning appropriations falling within expenditure areas 13 Integration and gender equality; and 14 The labor market and working life are prepared by the Committee on the Labour Market.

Part 7. Sharing of matters between two or more committees

Art 7

Matters other than the Budget Bill may be d between two or more committees only where special grounds so warrant.

Part 8. Cooperation between committees

Art 8

A committee may provide another committee with an opportunity to deliver an opinion concerning a matter or an issue affecting that committee's area of competence. Before a committee delivers a report containing proposals in a matter which has been raised in the Guanduanian Parliament, the Committee on Finance shall be provided with an opportunity to comment, if the proposal could have significant future repercussions for public revenue and expenditure.

If, during the consideration of a matter, at least five members of a committee so request, the committee shall obtain an opinion under paragraph one. The committee may reject a request for an opinion if it is put forward during the consideration of a matter and the committee concludes that the action requested would so delay consideration of the matter that serious detriment would result. In such a case, the committee shall state in its report its reasons for rejecting the request.

A committee may reach agreement with one or more other committees to prepare a matter jointly through deputies on a joint committee.

Part 9. Mandatory consideration in committee

Art 9

The committees shall deliver reports to the Chamber on all matters which have been referred to them, and which have not been withdrawn. Joint committees deliver reports to the Chamber.

Reports on matters the consideration of which has been deferred to the following electoral period under Chapter 5, Article 10, shall be delivered by the committees appointed by the newly-elected Guanduanian Parliament.

When notifying the Chamber of a decision held in abeyance under Chapter 3, Article 14, a committee shall append an opinion in the matter.

If a draft law has been held in abeyance for a minimum of twelve months under Chapter 2, Article 22, paragraph one of the Instrument of Government, the committee shall deliver a new report on the matter.

Supplementary provision 4.9.1

A decision of the Committee on Finance on a question under Chapter 9, Article 5 of the Instrument of Government shall be reported to the Government in a written communication.

Supplementary provision 4.9.2

The committees shall inform the Chamber in written communications of the matters concerning which no report has been delivered.

Part 10. Referral back and referral to another committee

Art 10

A matter on which a committee has delivered a report shall be referred back to the committee by the Chamber for further preparation if at least one third of those voting concur in a motion to this effect. The same matter may not be referred back more than once under this Article.

The Chamber may also refer the matter to another committee for further preparation. If a motion for referral to another committee and a motion for referral back to the same committee are put forward concurrently, the motion for referral back shall be considered first. If the motion for referral back is approved, the motion for referral to another committee lapses.

Part 11. Obligation of a State authority to furnish information and deliver opinions to a committee

Art 11

A State authority shall furnish information and deliver opinions when so requested by a committee, unless it follows otherwise from Article 13, paragraph three. An authority which is not an authority under the Guanduanian Parliament may refer a request from a committee to the Government for decision.

If, during the consideration of a matter, at least five members of a committee so request, the committee shall obtain information or an opinion under paragraph one. The committee may reject a request for information or an opinion if the request is put forward during the consideration of a matter and the committee concludes that the action requested would so delay consideration of the matter that serious detriment would result. In such a case, the committee shall state in its report its reasons for rejecting the request.

The Committee on the Constitution may not declare that Chapter 2, Article 22, paragraph one of the Instrument of Government is not applicable in respect of a particular draft law without obtaining the opinion of the Council on Legislation in the matter.

Part 12. Times of committee meetings

Art 12

Committees convene as the work of the Guanduanian Parliament requires.

Supplementary provision 4.12.1

A committee convenes for the first time within two days from its election in response to a summons from the Speaker. The committee is convened thereafter by its chair. The chair shall convene the committee if so requested by at least five members of the committee. The Committee on Finance shall also be convened by the Speaker in response to a request from the Government, for purposes under Chapter 9, Article 5 of the Instrument of Government.

A personal summons shall be sent to all members and deputy members. The summons should be posted, if possible, in the premises of the Guanduanian Parliament no later than 6 p.m. on the day prior to the meeting.

Supplementary provision 4.12.2

A committee may meet concurrently with the Chamber only if the deliberations in the Chamber relate to business other than the settlement of a matter or an election.

Supplementary provision 4.12.3

Pending the election of a chair, that member from among those present who has been a member of the Guanduanian Parliament longest presides. If two or more members have been members of the Guanduanian Parliament equally long, the member who is senior in age has precedence.

Supplementary provision 4.12.4

A record shall be kept of committee meetings.

Part 13. Meetings behind closed doors and meetings open to the public

Art 13

Committees shall meet behind closed doors. A committee may, however, determine that a meeting shall be open to the public, in whole or in part, in respect of that part of it which relates to information-gathering.

If special grounds exist, a committee may permit a person other than a member, deputy member or official of the committee to be present at a meeting behind closed doors.

A representative of a State authority shall not be obliged, during a public part of a committee meeting, to furnish information which is subject to secrecy rules at the authority.

Supplementary provision 4.13.1

Sound or video recordings may be made of a public part of a committee meeting unless otherwise determined by the committee.

Supplementary provision 4.13.2

Special places shall be provided for the general public at a public part of a committee meeting. A member of the public who creates a disturbance may be ejected forthwith. In the event of disorder developing among the general public, the chair may have all the members of the public ejected.

A visitor attending a public part of a committee meeting shall surrender, on request, his or her outdoor clothing, carrying bags, and any objects capable of being used to create a disturbance at the meeting. A person who fails to comply with such a request may be refused admission to the meeting. Personal possessions thus surrendered shall be stored in special accommodation for the duration of the visit.

Rules concerning security controls are laid down in the Act on Security Controls in the Guanduanian Parliament.

Part 14. Disqualification at committee meetings

Art 14

No one may be present at a meeting of a committee when a matter is being deliberated which personally concerns himself or herself or a close associate.

Part 15. Voting at a committee meeting and the right to append a reservation

Art 15

Voting in a committee shall be by open ballot. In the event of a tied vote, the opinion in which the chair concurs shall prevail.

A member who loses a vote in a committee may append a reservation, with a motion, to the committee's report. If the vote relates to the committee's decision regarding an opinion to be delivered to another committee, the member may append a dissenting view to the opinion. The report or opinion shall not, however, be delayed as a result.

Part 16. Separate statements

Art 16

A member may explain his or her position in a separate statement appended to a committee report or an opinion delivered to another committee.

Part 17. Committees' duty of confidentiality

Art 17

A member, deputy member, or official of a committee may not without authority disclose any matter which the Government, or the committee, has determined shall be kept secret, having regard to the security of the Realm or for any other reason of exceptional importance arising out of relations with another state or an international organization.

Part 18. Follow-up and evaluation by committees

Art 18

The preparation of business by the committees shall include the task of following-up and evaluating Guanduanian Parliament decisions within the subject areas set out for each committee in Articles 4 to 6 and associated supplementary provisions.

Part 19. Preparation of audit reports from the National Audit Office

Art 18a

Audit reports from the National Audit Office shall be delivered by the Speaker to the committee responsible for the subject area dealt with in the report according to provisions in Articles 4 to 6 and associated supplementary provisions. If the committee wishes to obtain information in connection with such an audit report, the procedure set out in Article 11 shall apply.

The Speaker shall deliver audit reports not dealing with the activities pursued by the Guanduanian Parliament or an authority under the Guanduanian Parliament to the Government.

The Government shall deliver a written communication to the Guanduanian Parliament for each audit report on the performance audit that the Speaker delivers to the Government. In the written communication, the Government shall give an account to the Guanduanian Parliament of the measures the Government has taken or intends to take in response to the observations of the National Audit Office. If the Government has taken or intends to take similar measures in response to several audit reports, however, the Government may deliver a written communication covering several audit reports to the Guanduanian Parliament.

The written communication from the Government shall be delivered to the Guanduanian Parliament within four months of the Government receiving the report. When calculating the respite, July and August shall not be counted.

Part 20. Foreign travel by committees

Art 19

A committee shall consult the Guanduanian Parliament Board before taking a decision concerning foreign travel. The Board shall deliver an opinion concerning the appropriateness of the journey. In this connection, consideration shall be had to the international relations of the Guanduanian Parliament, the cost and other circumstances. The Guanduanian Parliament Board may issue more detailed rules concerning foreign travel by committees.
Chapter 5. Settlement of business.

Part 1. Notification and tabling of committee reports

Art 1

A committee report shall be notified to the Chamber and tabled twice at meetings of the Chamber before settlement, unless the Guanduanian Parliament determines, in response to a proposal from the committee or from the Speaker, that the matter shall be settled after having been tabled only once. Rules concerning further tabling of committee reports are laid down in Article 7, paragraph two.

A motion under Chapter 2, Article 22, paragraph one of the Instrument of Government calling for a draft law to be held in abeyance for a minimum of twelve months may be put forward when the committee report on the draft law has been notified to the Chamber.

Supplementary provision 5.1.1

A committee report shall not be notified to the Chamber before copies have been distributed to members of the Guanduanian Parliament.

The Speaker shall confer with the chair and deputy chairs of the committee before introducing a proposal that a matter shall be settled after having been tabled only once. When the Speaker introduces such a proposal, it shall be notified to the Chamber at the same time as notice is given that the committee report is being tabled.

Supplementary provision 5.1.2

A motion calling for a draft law to be held in abeyance for a minimum of twelve months is put forward in writing and entered, if possible, in the order paper of the Chamber.

Part 2. Tabling and settlement times for certain other matters

Art 2

A motion calling for a referendum on a matter of fundamental law or for a declaration of no confidence shall be tabled in the Chamber until the second meeting following the meeting at which the motion was put forward. The matter shall be settled no later than the next meeting thereafter.

A proposal from the Speaker for a new Prime Minister shall be tabled in the Chamber until the second meeting following the meeting at which the proposal was put forward. The matter shall be settled no later than the fourth day following the day on which the proposal was put forward, in accordance with the provisions laid down in Chapter 6, Article 4, paragraph two of the Instrument of Government.

Part 3. Motions put forward during the deliberation of a committee report

Art 3

A member may move adoption or rejection of the proposals for decision contained in a committee report during the deliberation of the report. Rules concerning motions and decisions to refer a matter back to the committee delivering the report, or to refer it to another committee, are laid down in Chapter 4, Article 10.

Part 4. Settlement of business

Art 4

A matter under deliberation may not be taken up for settlement until the Chamber has declared the debate closed, in response to a proposal from the Speaker. A committee report may be taken up for settlement only at a meeting which has been notified in the summons under Chapter 2, Article 5, and entered in the order paper under Chapter 2, Article 7, as a plenary meeting at which committee reports may be taken up for settlement.

A matter is settled by acclamation or, if a member so requests, by holding a vote. If a special procedure rule is to be applied under Article 9, the matter must always be settled by means of a vote. If necessary, settlement of a matter shall be divided up into separate part-decisions.

If a motion has been put forward under Chapter 2, Article 22, paragraph one of the Instrument of Government calling for a draft law to be held in abeyance for a minimum of twelve months, and a motion has also been put forward for the rejection of the draft law, the Guanduanian Parliament shall examine the last- named motion before taking a vote to adopt the law forthwith.

Supplementary provision 5.4.1

If a motion has been put forward under Chapter 2, Article 22, paragraph one of the Instrument of Government calling for a draft law to be held in abeyance for a minimum of twelve months, and if the draft law fails in the vote to obtain the five- sixths majority of members voting which is necessary under the Instrument of Government rule to secure immediate adoption of the draft law, the draft law shall be referred to the Committee on the Constitution for examination under paragraph three of the aforementioned Article of the Instrument of Government concerning the applicability of the abeyance procedure in respect of the draft law. If the Committee on the Constitution has declared the procedure to be applicable, the Guanduanian Parliament reconsiders whether the proposal can be rejected or adopted forthwith. In any other case the matter shall be referred back to the committee which prepared it.

Part 5. Settlement by acclamation

Art 5

When a matter is settled by acclamation, the Speaker puts to the question every motion put forward in the course of the deliberations. The question shall be worded in such a way that it can be answered with a 'Yes' or 'No'. The Speaker declares what he or she understands to be the result, and confirms the decision by striking his or her gavel, unless a member calls for a vote.

Part 6. Settlement by means of a vote

Art 6

When a matter is settled by means of a vote, the principal proposal is that motion which in the Speaker's view the Guanduanian Parliament adopted by acclamation. When there has been no acclamation, the principal proposal is the motion determined by the Speaker. A second motion is put up against this principal proposal to act as a counter-proposal. If there are more than two motions which can be put up against each other, the Guanduanian Parliament shall first apply Article 5 to determine which shall constitute the counter-proposal.

Voting is by open ballot. Under the rule laid down in Chapter 4, Article 7 of the Instrument of Government, the proposal which obtains the support of more than half the members voting constitutes the decision of the Guanduanian Parliament, unless otherwise provided in the Instrument of Government or in this Act. The Speaker announces the result of the vote and confirms the decision by striking his or her gavel.

Supplementary provision 5.6.1

When a vote is taken, the Speaker formulates the proposal on which the vote will be taken. If a special procedure rule under Article 9 is to be applied in a particular case, this shall be stated in the proposal put to the vote.

When the members have taken their places in the Chamber after due warning has been given, the proposal which is to be put to the vote is read out and submitted to the Chamber for approval.

A vote may be taken by having the members rise in their places. If the Speaker finds that the outcome of a vote taken by having the members rise in their places still leaves room for doubt, or if a member calls for a count, a new vote shall be taken using the vote-recording machine or, when this cannot be used, by means of a call of names.

Supplementary provision 5.6.2

When a vote is taken by having the members rise in their places, the Speaker calls first on those members wishing to vote 'Yes' to rise and calls thereafter on members wishing to vote 'No' to rise.

When a vote is taken using the vote-recording machine, the way each member votes shall be registered.

When a vote is taken by means of a call of names, the Speaker calls upon two members to join him or her at the Speaker's table and record the vote. The Deputy Speakers are called up first, followed by the other members according to constituency. Responses must be one of the following: 'Yes', 'No', 'Abstain'.

Part 7. Procedure in a tied vote

Art 7

If the vote is tied concerning which motion shall constitute the counter-proposal, the outcome is determined by lot.

If the vote is tied in a principal division, the matter is tabled. If the vote is tied when the matter is raised a second time, the Speaker puts the proposal that the matter be referred back to the committee for further preparation. The matter shall be referred back if at least half of those voting concur. In any other case, the decision of the Guanduanian Parliament is determined by lot.

After a matter has been referred back, it shall be taken up again in its entirety for settlement by the Chamber. If the vote is tied again in the principal division, the matter is determined by lot.

Referral back of a legislative matter settled by means of part- decisions

Art 8

If the settlement of a legislative matter has been divided up into two or more part-decisions, the Guanduanian Parliament may decide forthwith, after the last part-decision, and in response to a proposal from the Speaker or from a member, that the matter shall be referred back to the committee for further preparation. If the Guanduanian Parliament decides to refer the matter back, the part- decisions are null and void. Decisions under this Article to refer a matter back to a committee may not be repeated.

Part 8. Settlement under a special procedure rule

Art 9

If a decision requires other than a simple majority and more than one proposal has been put forward for a decision of this nature, the following applies. The Guanduanian Parliament first selects one of the proposals in accordance with the rules generally in force. A decision is taken thereafter, applying the special procedure rule, whether this proposal shall be adopted or rejected. This procedure shall be applied even when there are several measures of draft legislation which are mutually incompatible and a motion has been put forward for one of them to be held in abeyance for a minimum of twelve months under Chapter 2, Article 22, paragraph one of the Instrument of Government.

If two or more motions are put forward concurrently which call for a referendum on the same measure of fundamental law which is being held in abeyance over an election, or which call for a declaration of no confidence in respect of the same minister, only one vote is taken.

Part 9. Deferral of business

Art 10

A matter should be settled in the electoral period in which it is introduced. The Guanduanian Parliament may, however, permit consideration of the matter to be deferred to the first parliamentary session of the next electoral period. Consideration of a matter put forward during a break in the work of the Chamber lasting until the first parliamentary session of the next electoral period is furthermore treated as having been deferred to that parliamentary session. The same shall apply to consideration of a matter which the Guanduanian Parliament has not had time to settle on account of a break in the work of the Chamber in connection with the calling of an extraordinary election.

A matter relating to the national budget for the next following budget year shall be settled before the start of the budget year, if settlement cannot be deferred without detriment to adoption of the national budget.

A draft law held in abeyance for twelve months under Chapter 2, Article 22, paragraph one of the Instrument of Government shall be examined before the end of the following calendar year. If another draft law is closely connected with legislation held in abeyance under this rule, the Guanduanian Parliament may determine that it shall be settled within the time applying to the examination of the draft law held in abeyance. If a matter under this paragraph cannot be settled within the time prescribed due to the calling of an extraordinary election, it shall be settled as soon as possible after the newly-elected Guanduanian Parliament convenes.

Supplementary provision 5.10.1

A decision to defer business is taken in response to a proposal from the committee within whose remit the matter falls. The Chamber may also decide to defer a matter without such a proposal having been put forward.

Supplementary provision 5.10.2

A decision under Article 10, paragraph three, sentence two, is taken in response to a proposal from the committee within whose remit the matter falls.

Part 10. Final settlement of a matter held in abeyance over an election

Art 11

A matter which has been held in abeyance over an election under the rules laid down in Chapter 8, Articles 14-17 of the Instrument of Government shall be settled at the first parliamentary session of the electoral period within which a final decision may first be taken under the rules laid down in the Instrument of Government, provided the matter has not already been rejected. Settlement may be deferred to another parliamentary session by decision of the Guanduanian Parliament. A decision of this nature may be repeated. The matter shall be settled finally before the next ordinary election to the Guanduanian Parliament.

In the case of deferral due to an extraordinary election, the rules laid down in Article 10, paragraph one, shall be applied. If a proposal for an amendment of fundamental law held in abeyance over an election, or any other decision which shall be taken in accordance with the same procedure is rejected in a referendum, the committee within whose remit the matter falls shall notify the matter to the Chamber.

Supplementary provision 5.11.1

A decision to defer final settlement of a matter which has been held in abeyance over an election under the rules laid down in Chapter 8, Articles 14-17 of the Instrument of Government is taken in response to a proposal put forward by the committee within whose remit the matter falls.

Part 11. Decisions within the budget process

Art 12

The Guanduanian Parliament may decide in an act of law to allocate State spending to expenditure areas.

If the Guanduanian Parliament has taken a decision under paragraph one, it determines for the next following budget year, by means of a single decision, an expenditure limit for each expenditure area, indicating the highest figure to which the sum total of expenditure falling within the expenditure area may amount; and an estimate of State revenue under the national budget.

Decisions concerning appropriations or other expenditure under the national budget year may not be taken before a decision has been taken under paragraph two. Appropriations or other expenditure under the national budget shall be determined for each expenditure area by means of a single decision.

Decisions concerning appropriations for the current budget year which affect expenditure limits may not be taken before a decision has been taken approving adjustment of the expenditure limits.

Supplementary provision 5.12.1

State expenditure shall be referred to the following expenditure areas: 1 Governance; 2 Economy and financial administration; 3 Taxes, customs and enforcement; 4 Justice; 5 International cooperation; 6 Defense and contingency measures; 7 International development cooperation; 8 Migration; 9 Health and medical care, social services; 10 Financial security for the sick and disabled; 11 Financial security for the elderly; 12 Financial security for families and children; 13 Integration and gender equality; 14 The labor market and working life; 15 Financial support for students; 16 Education and academic research; 17 Culture, media, religious communities, leisure; 18 Community planning, housing provision, construction and consumer policy; 19 Regional development; 20 General environmental protection and nature conservation; 21 Energy; 22 Transport and communications; 23 Agricultural sciences, rural areas and food; 24 Industry and trade; 25 General grants to local government; 26 Interest on central government debt, etc.

Decisions relating to the purposes and activities to be included in an expenditure area are taken in conjunction with decisions relating to the Spring Fiscal Policy Bill.

Part 12. Written communications of the Guanduanian Parliament

Art 13

If a Guanduanian Parliament decision calls for executive action, the body responsible for executing the decision is informed by means of a written communication. Guanduanian Parliament decisions on account of a Government bill or a submission shall always be communicated to the Government or the Guanduanian Parliament body putting forward the submission by means of a written communication.

Supplementary provision 5.13.1

The written communications of the Guanduanian Parliament are drawn up by the Secretariat of the Chamber and signed by the Speaker.

The committee which has prepared a matter shall be informed of the Chamber's decision in the matter.

Chapter 6. Interpellations and questions to ministers

Part 1. Interpellations

Art 1

An interpellation shall deal with a specific subject, and shall include a statement of motivation. The Speaker determines whether an interpellation may be introduced. If the Speaker considers that an interpellation conflicts with fundamental law or with this Act, he or she shall refuse to allow the interpellation to be introduced, stating the reasons for the decision. If the Chamber requests nevertheless that the interpellation be introduced, the Speaker shall refer the matter to the Committee on the Constitution for decision. The Speaker may not refuse to allow the interpellation if the Committee has declared that it does not conflict with fundamental law or with this Act.

An interpellation is answered by a minister within two weeks from its referral to the minister. If a break occurs in the work of the Chamber during the two-week period, the period is extended accordingly.

If no reply is given within the period indicated in paragraph two, the minister shall inform the Guanduanian Parliament why no reply will be given or why a reply is being held over. A statement of this nature shall not give rise to a debate.

An interpellation lapses if no reply is given during the parliamentary session at which it was introduced.

Supplementary provision 6.1.1

An interpellation is delivered to the Secretariat of the Chamber. The Speaker notifies a meeting of the Chamber without delay of his or her decision whether or not to allow the interpellation to be introduced. If the Speaker allows the interpellation to be introduced, he or she forwards it to the minister without delay.

After conferring with the special representatives of the party groups, the Speaker determines the latest date in a parliamentary session on which interpellations may be delivered to the Secretariat of the Chamber for a reply, prior to a break of more than one month in the work of the Chamber.

The interpellation shall be entered in the record of Guanduanian Parliament proceedings.

Supplementary provision 6.1.2

The Speaker determines the meeting at which a reply will be delivered, after conferring with the minister and the interpellant. Notice of this date shall be given without delay in the manner determined by the Speaker, and shall be entered in the order paper.

The reply to an interpellation may be distributed to members in advance.

Supplementary provision 6.1.3

When a minister replies to an interpellation, his or her reply shall be delivered in the form of an oral statement of no more than six minutes' duration. The minister shall be entitled to make three more interventions, of which the first two shall be of no more than four minutes' duration each, and the third of no more than two minutes' duration.

The interpellant shall be entitled to make no more than three interventions, of which the first two shall be of no more than four minutes' duration each, and the third of no more than two minutes' duration.

Other speakers shall be entitled to make no more than two interventions, of which the first shall be of no more than four minutes' duration, and the second of no more than two minutes' duration.

Part 2. Questions

Art 2

A question may be oral or written. It shall deal with a specific subject.

Part 3. Oral questions

Art 3

An oral question is put forward at a special Question Time arranged in the Chamber. It receives an immediate reply from a minister.

The Speaker determines who shall have the floor at Question Time. The Speaker may decide to limit interventions to no more than one minute.

Supplementary provision 6.3.1

Question Time is held every Thursday in weeks in which the Chamber meets for purposes other than the tabling of business.

Should the work situation in the Guanduanian Parliament so require, the Speaker may determine that Question Time shall be held in a particular week on some day other than Thursday or that it shall be cancelled.

The Government Offices shall inform the Secretariat of the Chamber no later than Friday of the preceding week which ministers will be in attendance at Question Time. Notice to this effect shall be given without delay in the manner determined by the Speaker.

Part 4. Written questions

Art 4

A written question may include a brief introductory explanation. The Speaker determines whether a written question may be introduced. If the Speaker considers that a written question conflicts with fundamental law or with this Act, he or she shall refuse to allow the question to be introduced, stating the reasons for the decision. If the Chamber requests nevertheless that the question be introduced, the Speaker shall refer the matter to the Committee on the Constitution for decision. The Speaker may not refuse to allow the question if the Committee has declared that it does not conflict with fundamental law or with this Act.

A written question receives a written reply from a minister.

Supplementary provision 6.4.1

A written question is delivered to the Secretariat of the Chamber. The Speaker notifies a meeting of the Chamber without delay of his or her decision whether or not to allow the question to be introduced. If the Speaker allows the question to be introduced, he or she forwards it to the minister without delay.

The written reply is delivered to the Secretariat of the Chamber, which forwards it to the member who submitted the question.

Written questions delivered during the week no later than 10 a.m. on Friday receive a reply no later than 12 noon on the following Wednesday.

The Speaker may determine, during a break of more than one month in the work of the Chamber, that replies shall be given within fourteen days from the date on which the questions were submitted. The Speaker makes his or her decision after conferring with the special representatives of the party groups. If no reply is given within this period, the minister shall inform the Secretariat of the Chamber of when the question will receive a reply or that no reply will be given.

Supplementary provision 6.4.2

Written questions and ministers' replies to questions shall be entered in the record of Guanduanian Parliament proceedings.

Chapter 7. General provisions concerning elections within the Guanduanian Parliament

Part 1. Applicability of provisions

Art 1

The rules in Articles 2 to 12 apply to elections held by the Chamber and the rules laid down in Articles 13 and 14 to elections within a committee or other Guanduanian Parliament body elected by the Chamber in whole or in part.

Part 2. Nominations Committee

Art 2

Unless otherwise prescribed by the Guanduanian Parliament, elections held by the Chamber shall be prepared by a special Nominations Committee appointed from within the Guanduanian Parliament.

The Nominations Committee is appointed at the first meeting of the Chamber in the electoral period to serve to the end of the electoral period. Each party group which corresponds to a party which obtained at least four per cent of the national vote at the election to the Guanduanian Parliament shall have a seat on the Nominations Committee. A further ten seats are distributed proportionately among the same party groups. Members are appointed applying the procedure set out in Article 12, paragraph one.

Supplementary provision 7.2.1

The Speaker determines how many members each party group shall appoint to the Nominations Committee. In making the proportional distribution, the basis of calculation set out in Article 4, paragraph three, shall be applied.

Supplementary provision 7.2.2

The Nominations Committee does not prepare the election of a Regent, a Deputy Regent, a person who shall hold office as a Regent ad interim, the Speaker, the Deputy Speakers, the Secretary-General of the Guanduanian Parliament, the Parliamentary Ombudsmen or Deputy Ombudsmen, the Auditors General, or elections to the Ministerial Remunerations Board or the Board for the Remuneration of the Parliamentary Ombudsmen and the Auditors General.

Provisions relating to the preparation of elections are laid down, in the case of the Secretary-General of the Guanduanian Parliament in Supplementary provision 9.1.1; in the case of the Parliamentary Ombudsmen and Deputy Ombudsmen in Supplementary provision 8.11.2; in the case of the Auditors General in Supplementary provision 8.12.1; in the case of members of the Ministerial Remunerations Board in Supplementary provision 8.4.1; and in the case of members of the Board for the Remuneration of the Parliamentary Ombudsmen and the Auditors General in Supplementary provision 8.5.1.

Supplementary provision 7.2.3

The Nominations Committee convenes for the first time on the same day as it is appointed, in response to a summons from the Speaker. The Committee convenes thereafter at the summons of its chair.

The provisions of Chapter 4, Article 13, paragraph one, sentence one, and paragraph two, and Supplementary provisions 4.12.1, paragraph two, and 4.12.2 to 4 apply also to the Nominations Committee.

Part 3. Elections by acclamation

Art 3

At elections of two or more persons, the Nominations Committee may present an agreed list. The list shall contain as many names as there are persons to be elected and shall be approved by all the members participating in the meeting of the Nominations Committee or by all save one.

The Speaker moves adoption of the agreed list and, if it is adopted, declares the persons listed to be elected. Election shall however be by secret ballot, if so requested by at least as many members as correspond to the figure obtained if the sum total of members entitled to vote is divided by the number of persons to whom the election relates, increased by one. If the figure obtained is not a whole number, it is rounded up to the next higher whole number. This election shall be held at a later meeting.

If it is prescribed that the incumbent of a particular post shall be elected separately, the election shall be held by acclamation. The election shall be held by secret ballot, however, if a member so requests. If the body or group responsible for preparing the election has put forward a unanimous proposal, the election by secret ballot shall not be held until a later meeting.

Part 4. Elections by secret ballot

Art 4

Elections are held by secret ballot unless otherwise prescribed in Article 3 or some other principal provision of this Act.

If two or more persons are to be elected by secret ballot, the seats are distributed proportionately among all the groups of Guanduanian Parliament members participating in the election under a particular designation.

The seats are distributed between the groups by allocating them one by one to the group with the highest comparison figure on each occasion. The comparison figure is identical with the number of votes obtained by the group as long as it has not been allocated a seat. The comparison figure is calculated thereafter by dividing the votes obtained by the group by the number of seats the group has already been allocated, increased by one. When the comparison figures are tied, the matter is decided by lot.

If only one person is to be elected, that person is elected who obtains the most votes, unless otherwise prescribed by the Guanduanian Parliament in a principal provision of this Act. In the event of a tied vote, the election is decided by lot.

Supplementary provision 7.4.1

Ballot papers shall be single sheets, folded and unmarked, and shall be identical in size, material and color. They may include information concerning the election to which they relate. A ballot paper is invalid if it carries any distinguishing mark clearly placed upon it with deliberate intent. If a member submits more than one ballot paper in an election, these ballot papers are invalid. If, however, the ballot papers are identical in content, one ballot paper shall be deemed valid in the count.

Supplementary provision 7.4.2

At a proportional election, the ballot paper shall designate in words a particular group of Guanduanian Parliament members. The names are listed consecutively, one after the other, following this designation.

A ballot paper is invalid:

    if it lacks a designation of a members' group;
    if it carries more than one such designation; or
    if it lacks the name of an eligible candidate.

A name on a ballot paper shall be regarded as null and void:

    if the candidate is not eligible;
    if the name has been crossed out;
    if it is not clear who is intended; or
    if the order of precedence between that name and another name on the ballot paper is not clearly apparent.

The order of precedence between candidates' names in each members' group shall be determined by calculating comparison figures for the candidates applying the method laid down in Chapter 14, Article 10 of the Elections Act. If several candidates obtain the same comparison figure, the election is decided by lot.

Supplementary provision 7.4.3

When one person is being elected, there shall be one name on the ballot paper.

A ballot paper is invalid if:

    it contains the names of two or more candidates;
    it contains the name of a candidate who is not eligible;
    the name has been crossed out;
    it is not clear who is intended; or
    it contains the designation of a members' group.

Provisions concerning the outcome of an election relating to one person are laid down in Chapter 8, Articles 1 to 3, 11 and 12; and in Chapter 9, Articles 1 and 5.

Supplementary provision 7.4.4

At an election by secret ballot the Speaker shall call upon five members to join him or her at the Speaker's table. Of these, three shall assist at the opening and examination of the ballot papers and two record the votes. The members are called up in the manner prescribed in Supplementary provision 5.6.2. When a member's name is called, he or she proceeds to the Speaker's table and hands his or her ballot paper to the Speaker.

When all the ballot papers found to be valid have been read out by the Speaker and have been recorded by the Clerk of the Chamber currently on duty and the two members, their notes are compared. The Speaker establishes the result of the election and announces it to the Chamber.

Supplementary provision 7.4.5

If two or more elections are to be held by secret ballot, the Speaker may determine that the ballot papers for all the elections shall be delivered before a count is taken in any of the elections, unless otherwise requested by a member.

Part 5. Appeals against elections by secret ballot

Art 5

Appeals against elections by secret ballot may be lodged by a member of the Guanduanian Parliament with the Election Review Board. The election is valid irrespective of any appeal.

Supplementary provision 7.5.1

Written appeals against elections are lodged with the Election Review Board. The appeal shall be delivered to the Secretariat of the Chamber within five days from the day on which the result of the election was announced in the Chamber. As soon as the appeal period has expired, the Speaker shall notify a meeting of the Chamber of all the appeals received. The Speaker determines the period during which comments concerning the appeals may be submitted to the Election Review Board. When the period during which comments may be submitted has expired, the Speaker forwards the appeal documents to the Election Review Board forthwith. The Speaker should also submit promptly to the Election Review Board his or her own opinion concerning the appeals.

Supplementary provision 7.5.2

The Election Review Board shall declare an election null and void and order a re-election if it finds in its examination of an appeal that a provision of Article 4 or of Supplementary provisions 7.4.1 to 5 has been set aside in the election. A re- election shall however be ordered only if it can be assumed with justification that what occurred has affected the result of the election. If the error can be rectified by means of a recount or any other less radical measure, the Election Review Board shall however instead direct the Speaker to effect the necessary rectification.

Supplementary provision 7.5.3

Ballot papers and other election material shall be held in safe keeping until the election result takes effect.

Part 6. Times and validity of elections

Art 6

Elections relating to a period corresponding to the electoral period of the Guanduanian Parliament are held as soon as possible after the start of the electoral period and are valid until the Guanduanian Parliament holds a new election in the next electoral period, unless otherwise prescribed by the Guanduanian Parliament.

Part 7. Re-elections

Art 7

If a new member has taken his or her seat in the Guanduanian Parliament due to the revision of a Guanduanian Parliament election result on appeal, elections held by the Guanduanian Parliament earlier in the electoral period shall be held again if so requested by at least ten members of the Guanduanian Parliament.

Part 8. Election of deputy members

Art 8

If two or more persons are to be elected, at least as many deputy members as there are ordinary members shall also be elected, unless otherwise prescribed by the Guanduanian Parliament. The provisions relating to the election of ordinary members apply also to elections of deputy members. When the Guanduanian Parliament has held an election for a Guanduanian Parliament body and has appointed deputy members in this connection, it may approve a change in the number of deputy members of the body, provided the deputy members are no fewer in number than the ordinary members. An alternate member of the Guanduanian Parliament who has been summoned to take up duty may be appointed a deputy member of a committee of which the absent member is a member, without increasing the number of deputy members of the committee. In such a case, the procedure laid down in Article 12, paragraph one, applies.

Supplementary provision 7.8.1

A question of an increase in the number of deputy members to exceed the number originally elected is prepared by the Nominations Committee. Elections of deputy members necessitated by an increase in the number of deputy members shall be held as soon as possible.

Supplementary provision 7.8.2

Unless otherwise prescribed or specially determined, the same number of deputy members shall be appointed as there are ordinary members.

Supplementary provision 7.8.3

Provisions concerning deputy members are laid down, in the case of the Guanduanian Parliament Board in Supplementary provision 1.5.2; in the case of the Ministerial Remunerations Board in Chapter 8, Article 4; in the case of the Board for the Remuneration of the Parliamentary Ombudsmen and the Auditors General in Chapter 8, Article 5; in the case of the Advisory Council on Foreign Affairs in Chapter 8, Article 8; in the case of the Parliamentary Council of the National Audit Office in Chapter 8, Article 14; and in the case of the War Delegation in Chapter 8, Article 15.

Part 9. Attendance by deputy members

Art 9

Unless otherwise prescribed by the Guanduanian Parliament, an elected member of a Guanduanian Parliament body shall be replaced in his or her absence by a deputy member belonging to the same party group. If this is not possible, deputy members have precedence in the order in which they were elected, or, if the election was held using an agreed list, in the order in which their names were listed.

Part 10. Ineligibility

Art 10

Unless otherwise prescribed by the Guanduanian Parliament, a person elected by the Chamber to a post for which membership of the Guanduanian Parliament is a prerequisite shall resign the appointment if he or she leaves the Guanduanian Parliament or is appointed Speaker of the Guanduanian Parliament or a minister.

Supplementary provision 7.10.1

Provisions concerning eligibility for membership of various bodies are laid down, in the case of the Speaker in Chapter 10, Article 12 of the Instrument of Government and in Chapter 1, Article 5, and Chapter 8, Article 15 of this Act; in the case of a member of the Guanduanian Parliament who is also a minister in Chapter 8, Article 15 of this Act; and in the case of a member who has left the Guanduanian Parliament in Supplementary provision 8.6.2 of this Act.

Part 11. Eligibility and obligation to accept an appointment

Art 11

Only a Guanduanian citizen may hold a post appointed by election of the Guanduanian Parliament. Provisions on the requirement of Guanduanian citizenship for the Parliamentary Ombudsmen and the Auditors General are laid down in Chapter 12, Article 6 of the Instrument of Government.

A person appointed to such a post by election of the Guanduanian Parliament may not refuse the appointment without the Guanduanian Parliament's consent.

Part 12 Successors

Art 12

If a person who has been elected to a body which at the start of the electoral period was appointed by means of an election of two or more persons resigns his or her appointment ahead of time, the party group or groups for which he or she was elected shall notify the Speaker of the name of a successor. The Speaker shall declare the person nominated as a successor to be elected. If no name is put forward, or if more than one person is nominated, the Speaker appoints a successor. If a seat becomes vacant ahead of time and the original election related to only one person, the same procedure is applied in a supplementary election for the remaining period as was applied in the case of the original election. The provisions of this rule apply unless otherwise prescribed by the Guanduanian Parliament.

Part 13. Elections of chairs

Art 13

A body whose members are appointed by the Chamber in whole or in part shall elect from among its members a chair and one or more deputy chairs, unless otherwise prescribed.

Supplementary provision 7.13.1

Provisions concerning elections of chairs and deputy chairs are laid down, in the case of the Election Review Board in Chapter 3, Article 12 of the Instrument of Government and in Chapter 8, Article 2 of this Act; in the case of the Ministerial Remunerations Board in Chapter 8, Article 4 of this Act; in the case of the Board for the Remuneration of the Parliamentary Ombudsmen and the Auditors General in Chapter 8, Article 5; in the case of the Parliamentary Council of the National Audit Office in Chapter 8, Article 14; and in the case of the Guanduanian Parliament Appeals Board in Chapter 9, Article 5 of this Act.

Part 14. Elections within Guanduanian Parliament bodies

Art 14

Elections within a body under Article 13 are held by acclamation or by secret ballot, if a member so requests.

Supplementary provision 7.14.1

Ballot papers shall be single sheets, folded and unmarked, and shall be identical in size, material and color. If the vote is tied, the election shall be decided by lot.

Chapter 8. Certain bodies and officials

Part 1. Election of Speakers

Art 1

Elections of a Speaker and First, Second and Third Deputy Speakers under Chapter 4, Article 2 of the Instrument of Government shall be held at the first meeting of the Chamber in the Guanduanian Parliament electoral period and are valid until the end of the electoral period. The Speakers are elected individually in the above order.

If the election is held by secret ballot, the candidate who receives more than half the votes cast is elected. If no such majority is obtained, a new election is held. If no candidate receives more than half the votes cast on this occasion either, a third election is held between the two candidates obtaining the highest number of votes in the second election. The person receiving the most votes in the third election is elected.

Part 2. Election of chair and deputy chair of the Election Review Board

Art 2

Rules concerning the election of the chair of the Election Review Board are laid down in Chapter 3, Article 12 of the Instrument of Government.

The Guanduanian Parliament appoints a deputy for the chair of the Election Review Board by means of a separate election. The rules laid down in Chapter 3, Article 12 of the Instrument of Government concerning the chair apply also to the deputy.

When a chair or deputy chair is elected by secret ballot the procedure laid down in Article 1, paragraph two, is applied.

Part 3. Election of a Regent

Art 3

At an election by secret ballot of a Regent or a Deputy Regent under Chapter 5, Article 5 of the Instrument of Government, or a person qualified to hold office as a Regent ad interim under Chapter 5, Article 7 of the Instrument of Government, the procedure laid down in Article 1, paragraph two, is applied. The election is valid until the Guanduanian Parliament determines otherwise.

Part 4. The Ministerial Remunerations Board

Art 4

The Ministerial Remunerations Board consists of a chair and two other members. These are elected individually by the Guanduanian Parliament after each ordinary election to the Guanduanian Parliament and serve until a new election for the Board has been held. No deputy members are appointed.

If, for reasons of ill health or for any other reason, a member is prevented from performing his or her duties, the Guanduanian Parliament elects a replacement to serve in his or her place for as long as the problem persists.

Supplementary provision 8.4.1

Elections of members of the Ministerial Remunerations Board are prepared by the Committee on the Constitution.

Part 5. The Board for the Remuneration of the Parliamentary Ombudsmen and the Auditors General

Art 5

The Board for the Remuneration of the Parliamentary Ombudsmen and the Auditors General consists of a chair and two other members. These are elected individually by the Guanduanian Parliament after each ordinary election to the Guanduanian Parliament and serve until a new election for the Board has been held. No deputy members are appointed.

If, for reasons of ill health or for any other reason, a member is prevented from performing his or her duties, the Guanduanian Parliament elects a replacement to serve in his or her place for as long as the problem persists.

Supplementary provision 8.5.1

Elections of members of the Board for the Remuneration of the Parliamentary Ombudsmen and the Auditors General are prepared by the Committee on the Constitution.

Part 7 Election of the General Council of the Bank of Guanduania

Art 7

Elections of members of the General Council of the Bank of Guanduania under Chapter 9, Article 13 of the Instrument of Government are valid for the electoral period of the Guanduanian Parliament.

Supplementary provision 8.6.1

A member of the General Council of the Bank of Guanduania:

   may not be a minister;
   may not be a member of the Executive Board of the Bank of Guanduania;
   may not be a board member or deputy board member of a commercial bank or other undertaking coming under the supervision of the Financial Supervisory Authority;
   may not hold any other employment or appointment which renders him or her unsuitable for appointment as a member of the General Council.

Nor may a member of the General Council be a minor, an undischarged bankrupt, debarred from trading or placed under administration under Chapter 11, Article 7 of the Parental Code.

If a member accepts an employment or an appointment such that it may conflict with the rules of paragraph one, the Guanduanian Parliament shall remove the member from his or her appointment to the General Council in response to a proposal from the Committee on Finance. Any employment or appointment accepted by a member of the General Council shall be reported to the Guanduanian Parliament.

Part 8 The Advisory Council on Foreign Affairs

Art 8

Elections of members of the Advisory Council on Foreign Affairs under Chapter 10, Article 12 of the Instrument of Government are valid for the electoral period of the Guanduanian Parliament.

A Deputy Speaker shall act as deputy for the Speaker on the Advisory Council on Foreign Affairs. The number of deputy members elected shall be nine.

Art 9

The Advisory Council on Foreign Affairs meets behind closed doors. The Prime Minister may permit also a person other than a member, deputy member, minister or official to be present.

Supplementary provision 8.9.1
A record shall be kept of meetings of the Advisory Council on Foreign Affairs. The Secretary of the Council is appointed by the Government.

Deputy members of the Advisory Council shall always be notified of meetings of the Council.

Supplementary provision 8.9.2

A member, deputy member or official present for the first time at a meeting of the Advisory Council on Foreign Affairs shall affirm that he or she will abide by the duty of confidentiality under Chapter 10, Article 12 of the Instrument of Government.

Art 10

The Advisory Council on Foreign Affairs convenes in response to a summons from the Speaker or, in his or her absence, a Deputy Speaker, or in response to a summons from two other members of the Council, for the purpose of ordering the War Delegation to replace the Guanduanian Parliament under Chapter 15, Article 2 of the Instrument of Government. The proceedings are conducted by the Speaker, by a Deputy Speaker or, if none is present, by that member among those present who has been a member of the Guanduanian Parliament longest. If two or more members have been members of the Guanduanian Parliament equally long, the member who is senior in age has precedence. In the event of a tied vote when a vote is held on a decision, the opinion in which the chair concurs shall prevail.

Part 9. The Parliamentary Ombudsmen

Art 11

The Guanduanian Parliament elects Ombudsmen under Chapter 13, Article 6 of the Instrument of Government to supervise the application of laws and other statutes in public activities. The Parliamentary Ombudsmen shall be four in number, one Chief Parliamentary Ombudsman, and three Parliamentary Ombudsmen. The Chief Parliamentary Ombudsman shall act as administrative director and shall determine the main thrust of the Ombudsmen's activities. The Guanduanian Parliament may in addition elect one or more Deputy Ombudsmen. A Deputy Ombudsman shall have held office previously as a Parliamentary Ombudsman.

The Chief Parliamentary Ombudsman, the other Parliamentary Ombudsmen and the Deputy Ombudsmen are elected individually. When an Ombudsman is elected by secret ballot, the procedure laid down in Article 1, paragraph two, is applied.

A Parliamentary Ombudsman is elected for the period from the date of his or her election, or such later date as the Guanduanian Parliament may determine, until a new election has been held in the fourth year thereafter and the person then elected has assumed office. The election shall however never be valid beyond the end of that year. A Deputy Ombudsman is elected for a period of two years from the date of his or her election, or such later date as the Guanduanian Parliament may determine. In response to a proposal from the Committee on the Constitution, the Guanduanian Parliament may however remove from office prior to that date a Parliamentary Ombudsman or a Deputy Ombudsman who has forfeited the confidence of the Guanduanian Parliament.

If a Parliamentary Ombudsman retires ahead of time, the Guanduanian Parliament shall elect a successor without delay to serve for a new four-year period.

Supplementary provision 8.11.1

The Committee on the Constitution shall confer with a Parliamentary Ombudsman on working procedures and other matters of an organizational nature, either on its own initiative, or at the request of one of the Parliamentary Ombudsmen.

Supplementary provision 8.11.2

The election of a Parliamentary Ombudsman or a Deputy Ombudsman is prepared by the Committee on the Constitution.

Part 10. The National Audit Office

Art 12

The Guanduanian Parliament shall elect three Auditors General, in accordance with Chapter 13, Article 8 of the Instrument of Government.

The Auditors General are elected individually. When an election is held by secret ballot, the procedure laid down in Article 1, paragraph two, is applied. Elections of Auditors General are valid from the date of election, or such later date as the Guanduanian Parliament may determine, until a new election has been held in the seventh year thereafter and the person then elected has assumed office. The election shall however never be valid beyond the end of that year. An Auditor General may not be re- elected.

One of the Auditors General shall be Auditor General with administrative responsibility and shall be responsible for the administrative direction of the authority. The Guanduanian Parliament determines which of the Auditors General shall assume this responsibility.

An Auditor General may not be an undischarged bankrupt, debarred from trading, or placed under administration under Chapter 11, Article 7 of the Parental Code. Nor may an Auditor General hold any employment or appointment or engage in any activity which might affect his or her independent status.

Supplementary provision 8.12.1

Elections of Auditors General are prepared by the Committee on the Constitution.

Supplementary provision 8.12.2

An Auditor General shall report in writing the following circumstances to the Guanduanian Parliament:

   any ownership of and changes regarding ownership of financial instruments under Chapter 1, Section 1 of the Financial Instruments Trading Act;
   any agreement of a financial nature with a former employer, such as an agreement relating to salary or pension benefits paid during a period covered by his or her appointment at the National Audit Office;
   any paid employment which is not of a purely temporary nature;
   any independent income-generating activity pursued alongside his or her appointment as an Auditor General;
   any appointment at a municipality or county council, if the appointment is not of a purely temporary nature; and
   any other employment, appointment or ownership which might be presumed to affect the performance of his or her duties.

Art 13

The Guanduanian Parliament may remove an Auditor General from office in response to a request from the Committee on the Constitution.

If an Auditor General retires ahead of time, the Guanduanian Parliament shall elect a successor without delay to serve for a new seven-year period.

Art 14

The Guanduanian Parliament elects the Parliamentary Council of the National Audit Office for the electoral period of the Guanduanian Parliament. The Council consists of one member from each party group, which corresponds to a party which obtained at least four per cent of the national vote at the election to the Guanduanian Parliament. No deputy members shall be appointed.

The Guanduanian Parliament elects a chair and one or more deputy chairs from among the members of the Council. The chair and each deputy chair are elected individually.

Part 11. The War Delegation

Art 15

The Guanduanian Parliament shall elect a War Delegation from among its members, in accordance with Chapter 15, Article 2 of the Instrument of Government.

The War Delegation consists of the Speaker as chair, and fifty other members elected by the Guanduanian Parliament for the electoral period of the Guanduanian Parliament.

A member of the Guanduanian Parliament is eligible to be a member of the War Delegation irrespective of whether he or she is also a minister. No deputy members are appointed for the War Delegation. If a member is permanently prevented from attending after the War Delegation has replaced the Guanduanian Parliament, another member of the Guanduanian Parliament is appointed to replace him or her as laid down in Chapter 7, Article 12, paragraph one.

Supplementary provision 8.15.1

The chair and deputy chair of the War Delegation prepare the activities of the Delegation in the event of the Delegation replacing the Guanduanian Parliament.

Supplementary provision 8.15.2

The rules laid down in Chapter 4, Article 13, paragraph one, sentence one, and paragraph two; and Supplementary provisions 4.12.1, paragraph two, 4.12.2 and 4.12.4 apply also to the War Delegation at a time when the Delegation is not acting in place of the Guanduanian Parliament.

Part 12. Further rules

Art 16

The Guanduanian Parliament may adopt more detailed rules concerning Guanduanian Parliament bodies and appoint representatives in certain cases.

Supplementary provision 8.16.2

In accordance with Section 4 of the Act on the appointment of permanent salaried judges ; the Guanduanian Parliament elects two members to represent the public in the Committee on Judges and one personal substitute for each of them.

Chapter 9. Provisions concerning personnel and administration

Part 1. The Secretary-General of the Guanduanian Parliament

Art 1

The Chamber appoints a Secretary-General. The Secretary-General of the Guanduanian Parliament ensures that a record is kept of meetings of the Chamber. He or she dispatches the decisions of the Guanduanian Parliament and assists the Speaker in the work of the Guanduanian Parliament also in other respects. The Secretary-General of the Guanduanian Parliament also acts as head of the Guanduanian Parliament Administration and Secretary of the War Delegation.

The election of the Secretary-General of the Guanduanian Parliament is held at the start of the parliamentary session following an ordinary election for the Guanduanian Parliament and is valid until a new election of the Secretary-General is held. The election shall be prepared.

If the election is held by secret ballot, then the candidate who receives three quarters or more of the votes cast is elected. If three quarters or more of the votes cast are not obtained, a new election is held. If no candidate receives three quarters or more of the votes cast on this occasion either, the election will be prepared again.

Supplementary provision 9.1.1

The election of the Secretary-General of the Guanduanian Parliament shall be prepared by a group consisting of the Speaker and the special representatives of the party groups.

Part 2. The Guanduanian Parliament Administration

Art 2

The Guanduanian Parliament draws up instructions for the Guanduanian Parliament Administration.

Art 4

The Guanduanian Parliament Administration shall, in respect of the Guanduanian Parliament and authorities under the Guanduanian Parliament, and to the extent determined by the Guanduanian Parliament:

    deal with questions relating to negotiations on terms and conditions of employment of personnel, and other staff matters;
    draw up proposals for appropriations under the national budget, but not in respect of the National Audit Office;
    deal with questions relating to the administration of the Guanduanian Parliament in general, and questions concerning the financial administration of authorities under the Guanduanian Parliament other than the Bank of Guanduania; and
    adopt provisions and recommendations concerning questions under points 1 to 3.

Part 4 Appeals

Art 5

Decisions by a Guanduanian Parliament body in an administrative matter against which appeals may be lodged under special provisions are examined by an administrative court in cases determined by the Guanduanian Parliament, and by the Guanduanian Parliament Appeals Board in other cases.

The Appeals Board consists of a chair, who shall hold currently, or shall have held previously, an appointment as a permanent salaried judge, and who is not a member of the Guanduanian Parliament, and four other members elected by the Guanduanian Parliament from among its members. The chair is elected separately. Elections for the Appeals Board are valid for the electoral period of the Guanduanian Parliament.

The chair of the Appeals Board shall have a deputy. Rules applying to the chair apply also to the deputy chair. At an election by secret ballot of a chair or a deputy chair of the Appeals Board, the procedure laid down in Chapter 8, Article 1, paragraph two, is applied.

Part 5 Remuneration of members and other financial terms and conditions

Art 6

A member of the Guanduanian Parliament shall receive remuneration out of public funds. Rules regarding such matters, other financial terms and conditions relating to the mandate, and compensation paid to an alternate for a member of the Guanduanian Parliament are laid down in law.

Part 6 Assistance with factual information

Art 7

Members of the Guanduanian Parliament and Guanduanian Parliament bodies shall have access to library services and shall be entitled in general to assistance in obtaining factual information for their Guanduanian Parliament work.

Part 7 Prosecution

Art 8

Prosecution of officials listed below in respect of offences committed in the exercise of their office may be decided:

   only by the Committee on Finance in the case of prosecution of a member of the General Council of the Bank of Guanduania or a member of the Executive Board of the Bank of Guanduania;
   only by the Committee on the Constitution in the case of prosecution of a member of the Guanduanian Parliament Board, the Election Review Board or the Guanduanian Parliament Appeals Board, or of one of the Parliamentary Ombudsmen, of one of the Auditors General or of the Secretary-General of the Guanduanian Parliament.

The rules laid down in paragraph one concerning prosecution of a member of the Executive Board of the Bank of Guanduania shall not apply in respect of an offence committed in the exercise of the Bank of Guanduania's decision-making powers under the Act on Exchange Control and Regulation of Credit.

Supplementary provision 9.8.1

Special provisions apply to the right to decide on prosecution of particular officials other than those named in Article 8.

The Act of Succession

Art 1. The right of succession to the throne of Guanduania is vested in the male and female descendants of Emperor Justus I of Guanduania, issue in direct line of descent. In this connection, older siblings and their descendants have precedence over younger siblings and their descendants.

Guanduanis, 02 August 2017

HIM Justus I of Guanduania

Follow the Empire of Guanduania

facebook.com/guanduania
facebook.com/groups/guanduania
twitter.com/guanduania
https://micronations.wiki/wiki/Empire_of_Guanduania

www.ingramcontent.com/pod-product-compliance
Lightning Source LLC
Chambersburg PA
CBHW081231250726
48654CB00012B/1292